Penguin Handbooks

Dartmoor for Walkers and Ri

Hugh Westacott was born in London in 1932 and moved to Epsom, Surrey, on the outbreak of the war. He was educated at Tiffin Boys' School, Kingston-upon-Thames, and the North-Western Polytechnic. He was for ten years the Deputy County Librarian of Buckinghamshire and has also worked as a librarian in Sutton, Croydon, Sheffield, Bradford and Brookline, Massachusetts. During the war he spent his holidays with his family in Colyton, east Devon, walking five miles to the sea and back again each day, and his love of walking stems from these experiences. He is now a freelance writer and lecturer and in 1979 he was commissioned by Penguin to write this series of footpath guides to every national park and official long-distance path. He has also written *The Walker's Handbook* (Penguin, second edition 1980) and two forthcoming books, *Long-Distance Paths: An International Directory* and *The Backpacker's Bible.* His other interests include the history of the Royal Navy in the eighteenth century and the writings of Evelyn Waugh. Hugh Westacott is married and has two daughters.

Mark Richards was born in 1949 in Chipping Norton, Oxfordshire. He was educated at Burford Grammar School before training for a farming career. He discovered the pleasures of hill walking through a local mountaineering club. He became friends with Alfred Wainwright, the creator of a unique series of pictorial guides to the fells of northern England, who encouraged him to produce a guide to the Cotswold Way, which was followed by guides to the North Cornish Coast Path and Offa's Dyke Path. For two years he produced a selection of hill walks for the *Climber and Rambler* magazine, and more recently he has contributed articles and illustrations to the *Great Outdoors* magazine and numerous walking books, culminating in the present series of Penguin footpath guides. As a member of various conservation organizations and a voluntary warden of the Cotswolds Area of Outstanding Natural Beauty, he is interested in communicating the need for the protection of environmental and community characteristics, particularly in rural areas. Mark Richards is happily married with two lively children, Alison and Daniel.

The Penguin Footpath Guides

To be published:

Already published:

Dartmoor for Walkers and Riders

H. D. Westacott

With maps by Mark Richards

Penguin Books

Penguin Books Ltd, Harmondsworth, Middlesex, England
Penguin Books, 625 Madison Avenue, New York, New York 10022, U.S.A.
Penguin Books Australia Ltd, Ringwood, Victoria, Australia
Penguin Books Canada Ltd, 2801 John Street, Markham, Ontario, Canada L3R 1B4
Penguin Books (N.Z.) Ltd, 182–190 Wairau Road, Auckland 10, New Zealand

First published 1983

Made and printed in Great Britain by
Richard Clay (The Chaucer Press) Ltd, Bungay, Suffolk
Set in Monophoto Univers

Contents

Contents

Acknowledgements

I should like to express my appreciation of the help given in the writing of this guide by Ian Mercer, the National Park Officer, and two members of his staff, Elizabeth Prince and Tom Hardman. Needless to say, the views expressed are my own and are not necessarily those of the National Park Committee or its officers. The faults are mine alone.

Thanks are again due to Mark Richards for the superb maps that are such a feature of the guide. They are based on the 1:25000 Ordnance Survey maps, with the sanction of the Controller of Her Majesty's Stationery Office (Crown copyright reserved).

My heartfelt thanks are also due to Pam Hall and Sue Baylis, who typed the manuscript so efficiently.

Introduction

The best way to see and experience Dartmoor is by walking or riding across it. Motorists who see the moor through their windscreens can admire the attractive scenery (although the best parts of Dartmoor are remote from roads), but its delectable landscape can be appreciated properly only by those who are prepared to get mud on their boots and feel the wind on their face as they puff to the top of a tor, to be enthralled by the wonderful view. Between two and three miles an hour is man's natural pace and this speed allows him to drink in all that lies before him and above all to remember what he sees, to be recollected in tranquillity for a long time to come.

The purpose of this guide, one of a series covering all the National Parks of Britain, is to assist readers to find their way around Dartmoor by using public rights of way and other recognized routes. Although written primarily for walkers, many of the routes are on bridleways and can be used by horse riders and pedal cyclists, although the terrain grading system (see p. 11) is applicable to walkers only. The walks and rides vary in length from $4\frac{1}{2}$ miles to 22 miles, so that there are walks to appeal to motorists who want a short half-day stroll, to the more experienced family walker who is content with 8 or 9 miles, and to the hardened fell walker who wants a full day on the hills.

A great deal of thought has gone into the design and format of the guide to make it as easy to use as possible. Both the maps and the route descriptions are very detailed and great care has been taken to ensure that the relevant part of the text is always opposite the map to which it refers.

The maps

The maps are based on the 1:25000 (approximately $2\frac{1}{2}$ ins. to the mile) Ordnance Survey maps, updated and corrected by means of personal survey. Information not included on Ordnance Survey maps has been added, including the location of gates, stiles and signposts. A further refinement is that walls and fences are distinguished from each other. In order to keep the maps as legible as possible, contour lines have been omitted and hills have been indicated by tapered strokes, which gives a very clear idea of the shape of the landscape and should please those who find contour lines difficult to understand. The numbers shown on the line of the path enable the map to be cross-referenced to the appropriate numbered paragraph of the route description in the text. North is indicated on the maps but it is not necessarily at the top of the page. Grid lines are not shown on the maps themselves, but in the margins will be found the grid line numbers, allowing the maps in the guide to be used in conjunction with any edition of the Ordnance Survey maps.

The small-scale map at the beginning of the text of each walk will be useful for locating the start of each route. Beneath it will be found a profile of the path which shows how strenuous the climbs are. Mile points are shown on these maps.

A problem faced by all writers of footpath guides is how to cope with maps that are too large to fit on to one page. Rather than adopt the traditional solution of adjusting the scale to fit the page, thus losing much essential detail, the longer routes have been divided into sections and a map provided for each. The appropriate part of the route description always appears opposite the sectional map. Wherever possible, the maps have been drawn so that when they are held in the natural map-reading position, the path starts at the bottom of the page and runs upwards. The continuation of a route from one map to the next is indicated by the letters in the margin, A joining up with A, B with B and so on. In some instances the shape of the route requires that two separate sections of the walk should appear on the same map, and in these cases it will be necessary to turn back to the appropriate page. North is indicated on all the maps, so that it is easy to align the different sections of the route.

Route description

Great care has been taken to describe the routes as accurately and precisely as possible so that those who find maps something of a mystery may follow the path as easily as a competent map reader. But the countryside is always changing and the accuracy of the route descriptions can be guaranteed only at the precise moment that they were made. As far as possible the routes have been described in relation to objects and landmarks that are normally not subject to change, but the author cannot be held responsible if a new fence is erected or a house is repainted after the route has been surveyed.

Very occasionally paths are diverted from their original route by the National Park Department. When this occurs the new route will be indicated by waymarks and signposts and should always be followed. Readers are urged to report any cases of obstruction to the National Park Department, giving a brief description of the problem and its exact location, preferably with a grid reference.

The author of this guide would appreciate comments on any inaccuracies or ambiguities which will be corrected in later editions and the source acknowledged. Please write to him c/o Penguin Books Ltd, 536 King's Road, London SW10 0UH.

At the beginning of each walk will be found basic information about public transport, parking and the availability of refreshments. Readers are urged to carry sufficient food and drink with them, as cafés and public houses cannot always be relied on, especially out of season.

Grading of routes

In order to assist the walker to choose routes within his walking ability, they are graded according to the nature of the terrain and the amount of skill required to follow the route.

Grading of the terrain

Easy: Short routes over well-defined paths and tracks avoiding open moorland. There may be some short, steep climbs, but all these walks should be suitable for the inexperienced.

Moderately difficult: Routes over paths which at times may be indistinct but which follow clearly defined features such as walls, fences and streams. On some of these routes there are *short* stretches of open moorland where it may be wet and rough underfoot. These routes are not suitable for novices.

Difficult: Longer routes including considerable stretches of open moorland where no proper path exists and where the ground underfoot is likely to be broken, difficult and wet. These routes are suitable for experienced hill walkers only.

Route-finding grades

Easy: Routes over well-defined paths and tracks usually way-marked and signposted. No map-reading skills required and walkers should have no difficulty in following the routes from the instructions alone.

Moderately difficult: Routes over paths which may not be always visible on the ground and where it is necessary to follow obvious features such as walls, fences and streams. Occasionally a compass will be useful, but it is not essential if the route instructions are followed carefully.

Difficult: Routes over open country often where no path exists. Anyone using these routes must be skilled in the use of map and compass and always carry the 1:50000 or 1:63360 Tourist Map. Compass bearings are sometimes given in circumstances where no description will suffice.

The National Park

Dartmoor National Park, with an area of 365 sq. miles, was established in 1951 under the National Parks and Access to the Countryside Act. The National Park Authority is a committee of the Devon County Council and has the statutory duty of preserving and enhancing the natural beauty of the Park and the promotion of its enjoyment by the public. It must be understood by all those who seek recreation in the National Park that the land is still privately owned. It is in no sense nationalized, and the mere fact that it has been designated a

National Park confers no special rights or privileges to wander at will. Much of Dartmoor is owned by the Duchy of Cornwall, and H R H Prince of Wales is therefore one of the principal landowners. Most of the farms on the moor are tenanted. The National Park Committee is responsible for planning and has to steer a delicate course to reconcile the sometimes conflicting interests of recreation, farming, forestry and the use of the area by the military. Remember, too, that even the wildest parts of the moor are farmed, although there may be no visible crops. Sheep, cattle and the Dartmoor ponies play an important part in the economic life of the community and are always owned by someone – they are not wild creatures.

As part of its statutory duty to promote recreation, the National Park Committee publishes a series of interpretative books and leaflets which give a great deal of useful information about Dartmoor. A select bibliography will be found on pp. 30–31. The headquarters of the Dartmoor National Park is at Parke, Haytor Road, Bovey Tracey, Devon, TQ13 9JQ (telephone: Bovey Tracey 832093). In addition there are information centres at Postbridge and Princetown which are open during the summer months.

As part of its policy of interpreting Dartmoor life, the National Park organizes a series of guided walks, led by experts, in many parts of Dartmoor. For motorists new to walking, this is an excellent way of being introduced to Dartmoor and the delights of moorland walking. A leaflet giving complete details of the guided walks may be obtained from the National Park Headquarters and any of the information centres.

Rights of way

The present state of rights of way within the National Park is less than satisfactory. Under the 1949 National Parks and Access to the Countryside Act, local authorities had a duty to compile definitive maps of public right of way. When the definitive map was published, this was conclusive evidence in law for the existence of a right of way. Unfortunately, on Dartmoor many well-used tracks and paths were not recorded as rights of way and some have been recorded inaccurately. For example, on route 19 the path runs northwards along the East Dart River and continues in a dead straight line to Grey

Wethers through the middle of a very boggy hollow. It is obvious that the path never ran through the bog, and indeed there is a well-used path a little way to the west which zig-zags up the hill to Grey Wethers. There is another example near Bellever Tor, where a National Park signpost shows a non-existent route to Huccaby Ring. There is a perfectly clear path slightly to the east which runs past the standing stone, and this is almost certainly the correct line, although the maps show otherwise. There are numerous examples of well-used tracks which are not recorded on the definitive map. Among the most obvious is route 16 from Widecombe across Hameldown. A particularly odd example exists near Postbridge. The drift lane which Crossing mentions in his monumental *Guide to Dartmoor* is marked on the definitive map for part of its route, but in two fields it is not recorded at all, which means that theoretically there is no right of access to the open moor along this route.

It should be noted that all rights of way are subject to legal extinguishment and diversion. Whenever this happens the National Park waymarks the new route and walkers and riders should follow the diverted route in preference to the instructions contained in this guide.

Access on open moorland

Open moorland may be defined as those parts of the moor which are not enclosed with walls or fences. This includes much of the wilder parts of the moor which is not cultivated and is given over to the grazing of cattle, sheep and ponies. There is no *legal* right to wander at will (known as access) on the open moor except in one or two places where access agreements have been negotiated. There is, however, what is known as *de facto* (as distinct from *de jure*) access, which means that, although there is no absolute right to wander, the custom is hallowed by tradition and is generally permitted.

Access on open moorland is further complicated by the newtakes. Certain ancient farms on the moor were granted the right to enclose up to 8 acres of *good* land. Such enclosures are known as newtakes and occurred mainly in the eighteenth and early nineteenth century. In many cases considerably more than 8 acres were enclosed and the practice justified on the grounds that the additional acres were *poor* land. The National Park Authority maintains that there is no *de facto* access through newtakes, but there are many who believe that illegal enclosure cannot affect the traditional custom of access. In practice, walkers are unlikely to be challenged in the newtakes providing that they enclose only heather or rough pasture, but they should be entered only by gates and stiles. *On no account climb walls or fences.*

Common land

Numerous commons are marked on the Ordnance Survey maps. Only certain people are designated as commoners and the rights of common do not extend to the general public. The rights include grazing, turbary (the extraction of peat) and sometimes the taking of stones and rushes. There is no legal right of access to common land, but in practice a *de facto* tradition of access exists.

Public transport

There are good rail links to other parts of the country from Exeter, Torquay, Newton Abbot and Plymouth, but bus services on Dartmoor itself are somewhat limited, especially during the winter months. The National Park Department publishes annually a leaflet entitled 'Dartmoor Bus Services' which includes timetables for most of the summer services useful to walkers. However, it does not include some of the independent operators services nor the important service that runs between Tavistock and Okehampton. The Western National Bus Company publishes a comprehensive timetable covering all public transport services, including railway timetables for the whole of Devon. This is available for a fairly nominal charge from The Head Office, National House, Queen Street, Exeter EX4 3TF (telephone: Exeter 74191).

It should be noted that the National Park Department runs the Pony Express services. These mini-buses link some of the minor places on the moor during the summer months. Details of these services are included in the leaflet referred to published by the National Park and also the Western National timetable.

Most buses will stop to set down or pick up passengers at any convenient point on Dartmoor.

Dangers

All extensive areas of wild hill country must be treated with respect, but there are probably fewer dangers on Dartmoor than in many others of the National Parks, largely because the climate is so much milder.

Apart from getting cold and wet, which can be avoided by wearing suitable clothing, the biggest danger is getting lost. On the easy and moderate routes, this is unlikely even in a sudden mist, because these routes normally follow well-defined paths. Should you get lost, retrace your steps to your last known position and start again. If a mist comes down, great care will be needed on those parts of the route where the path is undefined. Always know which direction you should be travelling and have a compass to confirm this. If hopelessly lost in a mist, it is probably a good plan to follow a stream, as this will be sure, in time, to bring you to lower ground and a road. Care will be needed because sometimes the terrain will be boggy. (Note that although it is always perfectly safe to follow a stream on Dartmoor, this is not necessarily true in National Parks in other parts of the country.)

In wet weather the inadequately clad walker may be in great danger of succumbing to exposure, which can occur in comparatively mild temperatures when he is soaked to the skin and there is a high wind. It is essential always to carry good waterproofs and spare warm clothing. Prudent walkers undertaking the difficult routes will leave a note of their route with some responsible person and notify that person that they have returned safely. Mishaps can befall even experienced walkers. Late one winter afternoon, after a 20-mile walk across the moor, I was hurrying to get back to my car before nightfall. I was tired and hungry and, instead of taking a compass bearing as I should, I thought I recognized a landmark and made for it. Soon I was walking over broken ground and this in itself should have warned me that I was going astray. There was a hard frost and a sprinkling of snow and I soon discovered that I could cross the bog by leaping from one tuft of cotton grass to the next. Unfortunately, one such tuft proved to be the back of a dead sheep and I sank to my chest in freezing water which had collected in an old disused leat. Fortunately I was properly dressed. By putting on my waterproofs I managed to keep reasonably warm until I got back to my car and changed my clothes. It was a salutary warning.

Mountain rescue

In the unlikely event of encountering somebody who needs to be rescued, make a note of the precise position of the injured person and go as quickly as possible to the nearest telephone, preferably leaving one of your party to stay with the patient. Dial 999, ask for the police and inform them of the location of the person and the nature of his injuries. The police will then tell you if they want you to take any further action.

The weather

Dartmoor can be very wet indeed and is subject to mists which can blot out the landscape for hours at a time. The temperature on the open moor is likely to be considerably lower than in the sheltered valleys and extra sweaters should always be taken. In winter the weather can be very severe and blizzards are quite common. Anyone tackling the more difficult walks in the book should always get an up-to-date weather forecast.

Firing ranges

It is most unfortunate that a considerable area of the moor north of the B3357, the Tavistock to Moretonhampstead road, is used by the army as a training ground and for artillery practice. Firing takes place throughout the year except during the month of August. But the ranges are not in use all the time and the details of the times of firing are advertised in the local press, at post offices, police stations and on range notice boards. The boundaries of the ranges are clearly marked by red and white posts and flags are flown at strategic points when firing is taking place. *Never under any circumstances enter the ranges when firing is due to take place.* A recorded message giving details of the week's firing arrangements can be obtained by telephoning Plymouth 701924, Exeter 70164, Torquay 24592 or Okehampton 2939. Wherever a route crosses a firing range, a note to that effect is placed at the head of the walk. The danger areas are marked on the Ordnance Survey map.

Kit and equipment

During the summer months the only requirements for the easy and moderate walks are stout shoes, a plastic or nylon raincoat, a rucksack for carrying food and drink, and a spare sweater. A plastic bag would be useful for covering this guide and the Ordnance Survey map. Those undertaking the difficult routes should be properly equipped for hill walking, with boots, cagoules and overtrousers as well as a rucksack for food, drink and spare clothes.

Maps and compass

Anyone planning to walk the moderate or difficult routes listed in this guide should also obtain a copy of the 1:63360 (1 in. to the mile) Tourist Map of Dartmoor, which is not nearly as detailed as the maps provided in this guide but will be found useful for setting the route in the context of the surrounding countryside.

Anyone venturing on to the open moorland should carry a compass and know how to use it. In one or two instances a compass bearing has been given in the guide to assist the walker to find the correct route. Note that these are magnetic bearings and were correct in 1980. The bearing decreases by half a degree in every 4 years.

Everyone using Dartmoor for recreation should be aware that irresponsible behaviour may put at risk livestock or crops and may adversely affect the welcome that those that follow you receive from local people.

Enjoy the countryside and respect its life and work
Guard against all risk of fire
Fasten all gates
Keep your dogs under close control
Keep to public paths across farmland

Introduction

Use gates and stiles to cross fences, hedges and walls
Leave livestock, crops and machinery alone
Take your litter home
Help to keep all water clean
Protect wildlife, plants and trees
Take special care on country roads
Make no unnecessary noise

Geology

Dartmoor can be likened to an upturned saucer on a table top. Between 300 and 400 million years ago, sedimentary rocks were formed by the action of the weather on the earth's crust. About 300 million years ago there was considerable movement of the earth's surface in south-west England which caused the sedimentary rocks to be heated sufficiently to turn into magma, or hot molten rocks, which were forced upwards through the sedimentary layer above it. The magma did not reach the earth's surface, but cooled into a vast layer of granite just below it. Geologists believe that the magma stretches from Dartmoor all the way through Cornwall to the Scilly Isles, and possibly beyond. Over countless millions of years, the rocks above the granite have weathered and eroded and have exposed the granite. Granite is a very hard rock. It consists of quartz, mica and felspar, and it is this last which decays with the action of the weather and turns into china clay. Properly dressed granite will not deteriorate. The characteristic tors or rocky outcrops which abound on Dartmoor are generally supposed to be formed by the action of the weather, particularly rain and frost, and this causes the granite to split and break up into smaller portions which results in the large piles of rocks to be found scattered round the bases of all the tors. These are known as clitters. Tin, copper, arsenic, wolfram, silver, lead, zinc and iron are all found in the veins left behind by the liquid magma and they have been mined for many centuries. Granite is a superb building material and there are numerous quarries where the stone was worked. There is now only one working quarry left on Dartmoor, at Merrivale.

Landscape

Dartmoor is the only extensive tract of wild country left in southern England and as a consequence has earned a reputation which is largely undeserved. The dreaded Grimpen Mires which Sir Arthur Conan Doyle described in *The Hound of the Baskervilles* do not exist, and the large bogs into which men and beasts are reputed to have disappeared without trace are equally fictitious. Nevertheless, the peat, which can be many feet deep and which covers large tracts of the moor, soaks up vast quantities of water like a sponge, and there are considerable areas of marshy or boggy ground, known as quakers, fen or feather beds. Some of these areas are very extensive, especially at Raybarrow Pool near Hound Tor, at Cranmere Pool, and at the Foxtor Mires near Whiteworks.

I am very fond of Dartmoor – it has a charm, intimacy and character all of its own – though perhaps it cannot be rated very highly in the scenic stakes of the National Parks. It has none of the high, distant views to be found in the Lake District, the Yorkshire Dales or the Brecon Beacons. This is because the hills that form Dartmoor are, on the whole, well rounded and not particularly steep, although there may be a scramble over the last 50 or 100 ft to the top of the tor. The hills themselves tend to be characterless and to look very like each other, but the summit tors, although relatively small in relation to the size of the hill, do assume individual shapes.

There are great contrasts in scenery, ranging from the thickly wooded Lustleigh Cleave and Teign Gorge to the wild heather covered slopes around Whiteworks on the northern half of the moor.

In recent years the Forestry Commission and the South-West Water Authority have considerably altered the face of parts of the moor. The Forestry Commission have extensive plantations of conifers around Bellever and Fernworthy, which are totally alien to the character of Dartmoor and whose existence is to be deplored. The Avon Reservoir, those at Burrator and Fernworthy and the small one at Swincombe seem to be less intrusive than the forests.

Archaeology

Dartmoor has been described as one of the richest arch-aeological sites in Western Europe. It is known that Dartmoor has been settled since at least 3500 B C and, by one of those accidents of history, the prehistoric sites tend to be located higher on the moor. The later medieval sites and the com-paratively recent mining areas occur lower down, thus not impinging upon the relics of prehistoric man. So rich is this area in prehistoric sites that no less than 2,000 hut circles are known, and they can be seen by any casual observer, in some places littering the moor.

It is probable that mesolithic man hunted on Dartmoor from about 15000 B C, but no tangible evidence has been found. The supposition is strong, as we know for certain that Dart-moor was not covered in ice during the Great Ice Age. There is, however, plenty of evidence of neolithic man who lived from, say, 3500 B C to 2000 B C. It was during this time that the work of clearing Dartmoor of forest began and there is archaeological evidence that early man set fire to the forest to drive out the game.

From the start of the Bronze Age, which lasted approximately from 2000 B C to 500 B C, we find evidence of dwellings. The Bronze Age people, also known as the Beaker Folk because of their distinctive pottery, built the many circular huts which can be seen all over the moor. Two particularly fine examples are on the southern side of the B3357 between Merrivale and Princetown, and the huge walled enclosure containing many huts at Grimspound. Unfortunately, owing to the acid nature of the soil, only pottery and stone implements have survived from this time; metal and bone is destroyed in the soil. Grims-pound is particularly interesting because the huts themselves are so complete that it is still possible to see the entrances and also because the compound is walled. The huts were con-structed by building a double circle of stones, about 3 or 4 ft high and perhaps 10 or 12 ft across. Then the interior was excavated to a depth of 2 or 3 ft and the soil used to fill the gap between the two stone circles. There was a central post with rafters spreading to the wall. The roof was covered with thatch, reed or turf. Probably the most complete hut is the famous beehive hut near the East Dart River, north of Postbridge. This is an isolated example and its age is unknown.

It was probably the Beaker Folk who built the numerous stone circles and stone rows and erected the menhirs or standing stones all over the moor. As these people left no written record behind, we can only speculate on the purpose of these structures, but there can be little doubt that they had religious or ritual significance. The stone circles are not particularly large and cannot compare with Avebury or Stonehenge but they are remarkable for the sheer number of them still existing. There is a fine example near Little Hound Tor (route 11), and the Grey Wethers between Postbridge and Fernworthy Forest (route 19) is particularly interesting as it is a double circle. There is another example of a stone circle on Hurston Ridge (route 18) which is associated with a double stone row. Over 70 stone rows have been recognized on Dartmoor and they range in length from about 35 yds to one in the Erme valley of almost half a mile (route 1). Again, the stones are not particularly large, ranging in height from about 6 ins. to 7 ft.

The menhirs, or standing stones, tend to be more dramatic, as they are often as high as 10 ft. Three good examples are to be seen on Beardown Tor (route 5), near Bellever Tor (route 22) and below White Tor (route 5).

There are a few Iron Age hill forts with earth and stone ramparts to be seen on the moor. A good example is at Hunter's Tor near Lustleigh (route 14).

Much of Dartmoor is covered with a system of low rounded banks built of earth or stone, sometimes running for several miles. They are known as reaves, and modern archaeologists believe that they are prehistoric field and territorial boundaries. It has been said that Dartmoor has the most extensive collection of field and territorial boundaries surviving in Western Europe. The best time to see them is early in the morning, late in the evening or when the ground is lightly covered with snow.

The Romans have left no impression on Dartmoor. We know that Exeter was the cantonal capital and we know that they mined tin in Cornwall, but there is no evidence of them here.

Dartmoor is not mentioned by name in the Domesday Book but some 37 of the manors whose land lies mostly on the moor are mentioned. On Hound Tor (route 15) are the remains of a medieval village. When excavated, it was found that underneath the stone houses are the remains of earlier wattle and turf houses.

One of the distinctive features of Dartmoor are the clapper bridges, which are made from huge slabs of dressed granite. There are those who believe that the earliest examples date from prehistoric times, but archaeologists discount this on the grounds that prehistoric man probably had little use for wheeled transport on Dartmoor. The best example on Dartmoor is at Postbridge (see routes 19, 20 and 21), which is believed to date from the thirteenth century.

Before the coming of the modern road system, Dartmoor must have been a difficult and dangerous place to traverse in bad weather. During the Middle Ages a number of stone crosses were erected to assist the traveller to find his way. A good example is Bennett's Cross in the little car park just east of Warren House Inn on the main road (routes 18 and 19), and there is a whole series of crosses still in situation on the track from Burrator Reservoir to Nun's Cross Farm (route 2).

Industrial Archaeology

Dartmoor has been worked for its minerals for well over 2,000 years. It had long been suspected that prehistoric man had mined on Dartmoor, but it was not until Lady Fox carried out excavations at Kes Tor just after the war that conclusive evidence was found. Her excavations uncovered an Iron Age smelter's house and workshop, which proved what had long been suspected.

Tin, a comparatively rare metal, has been found in large quantities on Dartmoor, which, particularly during the Middle Ages, was one of the most important centres of tin mining. We tend to think of tin as being used as a thin coating on steel to make modern tin cans in which food can be preserved. This, of course, is a comparatively recent process and in medieval times the metal was combined with copper to make bronze, with lead to make pewter, jewellery and drinking vessels, and also for solder. Lodes of tin-bearing rock were formed in the granite and covered by a layer of sedimentary rock. As the rock weathered and eroded, it exposed the tin ore which in turn became eroded, and the stones containing the ore were washed loose by the force of water and carried downstream. Being heavy, these stones were deposited on the outward sides of bends of streams, while the lighter stones were carried further downstream. The medieval tinners found the ore-bearing rocks on the banks of the streams and crushed them to a coarse powder, first in a primitive hand mill and then in later times in horse-driven crazing mills and by crushing stamps operated by a water mill. Once the ore was crushed, all the waste had to be removed, leaving the tin ore, usually known as black tin, behind. This was done by washing in fast-flowing streams which carried away the waste and left the heavier ore. The tin miners became extremely skilled in the art and went to the length of narrowing streams to make them flow faster. This can be seen quite clearly on the East Dart River at Sandyhole Pass. Plymouth itself owes its present importance to the tin miners – their activities silted the River Plym, so that it was no longer possible for ships to get as far upstream as Plympton, and the new town of Plymouth sprang up at the mouth of the river. When tin-bearing ore was discovered and there was no suitable stream near by, artificial leats or water courses were built to bring water to the site. These can be seen all over Dartmoor. However, it must be pointed out that not all leats were designed for this purpose and many of them were constructed to bring fresh water to farms, villages and ultimately the larger towns. Some of these are still in use, notably the Prison and Devonport Leats.

Once the ore or black tin had been extracted from the stone, it had to be converted to white tin by smelting. The earliest method was simply to place the black tin in a hole in the ground and then light a fire, so that when the fire had died down the pure tin could be taken from the ashes. This was a clumsy method, and later a crude furnace was constructed by building clay cones around the ore. A fire was lit under the clay cones and the molten tin dropped through the fire and collected in a hole. In about the fourteenth century a more efficient method was developed which remained in use until the nineteenth century. A blowing house was constructed near the banks of a stream or leat and a mill-race provided so that the water would turn a large water wheel which would activate bellows inside the blowing house. A granite furnace was constructed and the tin ore mixed with charcoal was placed in it. The bellows would very quickly heat the furnace and the molten tin dropped through the stone rafters which supported the fire and was then ladled into granite moulds. There is an almost inexhaustible supply of peat on Dartmoor and this was converted into charcoal by burning it in mounds sealed over with turf and mud.

In medieval times the tin ore was taken to one of the four stannary towns, Tavistock, Ashburton, Chagford and Plympton, where the metal was tested for purity and stamped. The tin miners conducted their affairs according to stringent rules and had a parliament or court where matters affecting tin mining were discussed. They even had their own prison, at Lydford. It appears that one of the meeting places of the stannary parliament was on Crockern Tor (route 23) and the practice of meeting there lingered on into the eighteenth century.

During the nineteenth century more efficient methods of mining involving direct digging were developed and steam power was used to crush the ore. The last tin was produced on Dartmoor in 1939 at the Birch Tor and Vitifor mines (route

19) near Warren House Inn, and the remains of the buildings and workings can still be seen.

During the nineteenth century there were some forty copper mines on Dartmoor, the most important being Wheal Friendship, near Mary Tavy. Iron was mined at Ilsington and at Shaugh, wolfram near Plympton, and lead, silver and zinc at Wheal Betsy, near Mary Tavy (route 8). This particular mine was about 700 ft deep and first a water wheel and then steam power were used to operate pumps to prevent it flooding. During the early nineteenth century this mine produced 300–400 tons of lead and 4,000–5,000 ounces of silver annually.

Granite is the most obvious natural material on Dartmoor and has been used from earliest times for building purposes. The first method of cutting and dressing granite was the wedge-and-groove method, in which a metal wedge was driven along the length of the block to make a groove, which was deepened until eventually the block split. This was exceedingly cumbersome and time-consuming, and in about 1800 the feather-and-tare method was developed. Holes were drilled along the line to be split by using a jumper, a long metal chisel held by one man and struck by another using a sledge-hammer. The jumper was gradually turned till the hole was complete. Tares or metal wedges were inserted into the hole and supported at the sides by curved pieces of metal called feathers. The tares were repeatedly struck by a sledge-hammer and eventually the rock would split. Granite was quarried on a large scale at Foggintor (route 3) and Haytor (route 15). It is still quarried at Merrivale.

Gunpowder was manufactured at Powder Mills near Two Bridges (route 23) and was used extensively in the quarrying industry. The mortar where the strength of the powder was tested can still be seen. The industry died out after the invention of dynamite.

Warrening was conducted on a large scale over many centuries on Dartmoor. Large mounds, known as pillow mounds or buries, often about 30 or 40 yds long, were constructed from stone and soil and rabbits were encouraged to breed in them. These were caught in nets, providing a source of meat.

Other industries which should be mentioned include the now disused china clay works at Redmires. Peat was extracted from all over the moor and at one time naphtha was extracted from peat at Dartmoor Prison. There was a glass factory at Meldon near Okehampton and an ice works at Sourton.

Agriculture and Forestry

The whole of Dartmoor is farmed, although crops are normally to be found only in the more sheltered lowland areas of the National Park. Sheep, cattle and ponies graze on even the highest parts of the moor. Every year considerable numbers of ponies are killed on the roads because visitors will insist on feeding them, despite the by-law and notices forbidding the practice. In summer the animals have plenty of food and it is quite wrong to encourage ponies to approach main roads in the hope of being fed. Even on the wildest parts of the moor it is important to keep dogs under proper control and prevent them chasing livestock.

Considerable areas of the moor have now been clothed in the Forestry Commission's ubiquitous sitka spruce and Norwegian pine. These forests have nothing to commend them; they are virtually devoid of wild life; they are gloomy and depressing and often conceal interesting archaeological remains. However, having perpetrated this outrage, the Forestry Commission does its best to allow the walker to see what has been done in the name of public interest. Many of the forests have good tracks through them, but care should be exercised when tree-felling is in operation.

Letter Boxes

Unofficial letter boxes are, I believe, a unique feature of the Dartmoor scene. The first was set up in 1854 at Cranmere Pool by James Perrott, the famous Dartmoor guide who left a large bottle in which gentlefolk could leave their visiting cards. Later this was replaced by a visitor's book in which ramblers would write their name and address. This letter box is now maintained by the National Park Authority, who also look after the one at Ducks Pool, built as a memorial to William Crossing.

However, this charming custom has now got completely out of hand and there are believed to be no less than 200 letter boxes scattered all over the moor, some of them in the most unlikely places. The visitor's book and rubber stamp for recording your visit are normally kept in an ammunition box and often hidden in a tor, so that they can take some considerable time to find. The National Park quite properly refuse to accept any responsibility for boxes other than the two that they maintain, and the existence and location of boxes passes by word of mouth. It seems that some people have a mania for visiting as many boxes as possible, and this has caused a considerable amount of damage. For example, a box was hidden in the old tinner's hut at Fishlake and then moved a few yards away. In the frenzy to discover the box, the tinner's hut has become severely damaged. Let us hope that the practice of establishing letter boxes will soon die.

Literary Associations

Despite its evocative atmosphere, Dartmoor has nurtured few great authors and no writer of the first rank has written about it as extensively as, say, Thomas Hardy has about Dorset. Eden Phillpotts has written a play and some novels about Dartmoor; John Galsworthy lived at Wingstone Farm near Manaton in 1906–23 and set some of his short stories on the moor; the poet Sidney Godolphin lived at Chagford and was killed there at the inn during the Civil War in 1643; Charles Kingsley was born at Holne vicarage in 1819; John Ford, the Elizabethan dramatist and poet, was born at Ilsington; Robert Herrick lived at, and was vicar of, Dean Prior (described by Rose Macaulay in *They Were Defeated*); L. A. G. Strong was born in Plymouth and his novel *Dewar Rides* is set on the moor; Conan Doyle used the Princetown area as a setting for *The Hound of the Baskervilles*. Henry Williamson, who wrote *Tarka the Otter* and *Salar the Salmon* and other novels with a Dartmoor setting, lived at Sticklepath, and Olive Parr, better known as Beatrice Chase, lived at Venton near Widecombe. Before the war she wrote several books, such as *From My Dartmoor Window*, which give a good picture of Dartmoor life. She is now almost completely forgotten, as the brand of eccentric and unhealthy catholicism she adopted in the later years of her life is now entirely out of fashion.

To my mind, the most engaging writer about Dartmoor is William Crossing. He was born in Plymouth in 1847 and devoted the whole of his life to exploring and writing about the moor. A reprint of the 1912 edition of his most important book, *The Guide to Dartmoor*, is still in print, published by David & Charles, and a copy should be in the library of every lover of Dartmoor. He describes in considerable detail every path and track and gives an account of some of the antiquities. He has a delightful Edwardian style and in one unforgettable passage advises the rambler to fill his boots with oats at night so that they will dry out and keep their shape. His other books include *A Hundred Years on Dartmoor, Gems in a Granite Setting* and *Amid Devonia's Alps*.

Book List

Footpath guides

Crossing, William, *Crossing's Guide to Dartmoor* (1912), David & Charles, 1981.

Dartmoor National Park Department, *Bus Away – Walk a Day in the Dartmoor National Park*, Dartmoor National Park Department, 1979.

Dartmoor National Park Department, Walks in the Dartmoor National Park, Dartmoor National Park Department: No. 1. *From Moretonhampstead, Manaton and Lustleigh*, 1977; No. 2. *South West Dartmoor*, 1979.

Le Messurier, Brian, *Dartmoor Walks for Motorists*, Warne, 1980.

Starkey, F. H., *Exploring Dartmoor: Twenty-One Middle-Distance Walks*, published by the author, High Orchard, Haytor Vale, Newton Abbot, Devon, 1981.

Starkey, F. H.,'*Exploring Dartmoor Again*, published by the author, High Orchard, Haytor Vale, Newton Abbot, Devon, 1981.

Westacott, Hugh Douglas, *Walks and Rides on Dartmoor*, Footpath Publications, 1977.

General

Crossing, William, *Amid Devonia's Alps: Wanderings and Adventures on Dartmoor* (1888), David & Charles, 1974.

Crossing, William, *One Hundred Years on Dartmoor* (1902), David & Charles, 1967.

Crossing, William, *Tales of the Dartmoor Pixies* (1890), F. Graham, 1968.

Deacon, Lois, *Dartmoor with a Difference*, Toucan Press, 1973.

Edmonds, E. A., and others, *Geology of the Country around Dartmoor*, HMSO, 1968.

Endle, Rufus, *Dartmoor Prison*, Bossiney Books, 1979.

Gant, Tom, *Discover Dartmoor*, Baron Jay, 1978.

Gibbons, Gavin, *South Devon, including Dartmoor*, Geographia, 1968.

Gill, Crispin, *Dartmoor*, David & Charles, 1976.

Gordon, Douglas, *Dartmoor in All its Moods* (1931), E P Publishing, 1976.

Gray, Mary, *Devon's Dartmoor*, revised edn, James Pike Ltd, 1975.

Greeves, Tom, *The Archaeology of Dartmoor*, Dartmoor National Park Department, 1978.

Griffiths, Grace, *The Days of my Freedom*, World's Work, 1978.

Gunnell, Clive, *My Dartmoor*, Bossiney Books, 1977.

Hall, Alison, *Dartmoor National Park: The Flowers of the Open Moor*, Dartmoor National Park Department, 1977.

Hall, Alison, *Dartmoor National Park: The Trees and Forests*, Dartmoor National Park Department, 1977.

Hall, John, *Dartmoor National Park: Outline of the Geology*, Dartmoor National Park Department, 1977.

Harris, Helen, *Industrial Archaeology of Dartmoor*, David & Charles, 1968.

Harvey, Leslie Arthur, and St Leger Gordon, D., *Dartmoor*, 3rd edn, Collins, 1977.

Hoskins, W. G., *National Park Guide*, H M S O, 1957.

Lowther, Kenneth Ernest, *Dartmoor*, Ward, Lock, 1979.

Newcombe, Lisa, *Dartmoor Country and Life*, Jarrolds, 1978.

Perkins, J. W., *Geology Explained: Dartmoor and the Tamar Valley*, David & Charles, 1972.

Pettit, Paul, *Prehistoric Dartmoor*, David & Charles, 1974.

Pevsner, Nikolaus, *Buildings of England: South Devon*, Penguin Books, 1952.

Rouse, G. D., *The New Forests of Dartmoor*, 2nd edn, H M S O, 1972.

St Leger Gordon, D., *Under Dartmoor Hills*, 2nd edn, Hale, 1973.

St Leger Gordon, Ruth E., *The Witchcraft and Folklore of Dartmoor*, 2nd edn, E P Publishing, 1973.

Smith, Vian, *Portrait of Dartmoor*, Hale, 1969.

Somers Cocks, J. Vernon, *The Dartmoor Bibliography*, Dartmoor Preservation Association, 1970. Supplement issued in 1974.

Westlake, Roy J., *Dartmoor*, Barton, 1973.

Worth, R. Hanson, *Worth's Dartmoor*, ed. G. M. Spoon, 2nd edn, David & Charles, 1967.

Guide and Route Maps

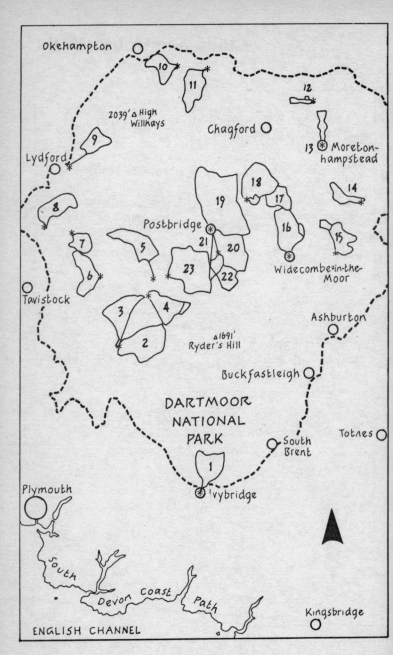

Okehampton

10 ✳
11 ✳
12

2039' △ High
Willhays

Chagford ○

13 ✳ Moreton-
hampstead

Lydford ✳

9

8

18
17
19
14

Postbridge ✳
16
15

7
5
21
20

6
23
22
Widecombe-in-the-
Moor

Tavistock

3 4
2

△1691'
Ryder's Hill

Ashburton ○

Buckfastleigh ○

DARTMOOR
NATIONAL
PARK

South
Brent ○

Totnes ○

1

✳ Ivybridge

Plymouth ○

South

Devon Coast Path

Kingsbridge ○

ENGLISH CHANNEL

KEY

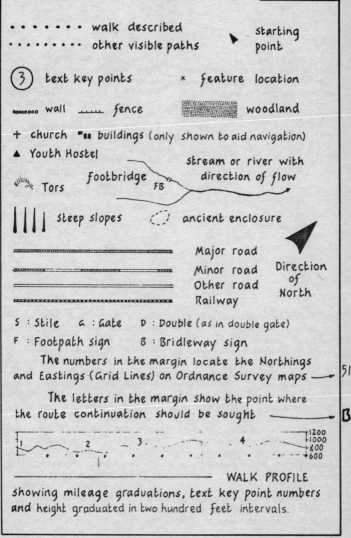

•••••••• walk described

•••••••• other visible paths

▼ starting point

③ text key points   × feature location

∘∘∘∘∘∘∘ wall   ..... fence   ▓▓▓▓▓ woodland

✝ church   ▪▪ buildings (only shown to aid navigation)

▲ Youth Hostel

〰 Tors   Footbridge   stream or river with direction of flow   FB

‖‖‖‖ steep slopes   ⟨⟩ ancient enclosure

▬▬▬▬▬▬ Major road

▬ ▬ ▬ ▬ Minor road

═══════ Other road

▬▬▬▬▬ Railway

◥ Direction of North

S : Stile   G : Gate   D : Double (as in double gate)

F : Footpath sign   B : Bridleway sign

The numbers in the margin locate the Northings and Eastings (Grid Lines) on Ordnance Survey maps —→ 51

The letters in the margin show the point where the route continuation should be sought ————→ B

WALK PROFILE

showing mileage graduations, text key point numbers and height graduated in two hundred feet intervals.

35

Route 1. Ivybridge, Hangershell Rock, Harford, Ivybridge

A route across open moorland by country lanes and field paths

Distance: 7 miles
For: Walkers (riders can complete the first half as far as Harford and then return to Ivybridge by road)

Terrain: Moderately difficult
Route-Finding: Moderately difficult
Maps: 1:50000 sheet 202; 1:25000 sheet S X65/75; 1:63360 Tourist Map
Start: Ivybridge, just off the A38, grid reference S X637562
Parking: Park in the large free car park at the top of the town near the bridge
Buses: Western National service 129 Plymouth to Exeter operates throughout year
Refreshments: There are public houses and a café in Ivybridge

1   The walk starts at the bridge at the top of the town. Follow the road up the right-hand bank of the River Erme (signposted 'Community College'), past the London Hotel, a mill and the Community College to the bridge across the railway. Cross the railway. After about 300 yards there is a bridle-way sign pointing along an enclosed track which runs beside Stowford Cottage on the right-hand side of the road. Just past the cottage the track turns sharp left and runs up the hillside to reach a gate which gives access to the open moor.

2   Take the broad grassy path which runs through the bracken bearing slightly away from the wall on your left. After nearly ½ mile, the path meets the old tramway track coming in from the right. This still has a little ballast left on it. Turn left, follow it for about 100 yds, then bear right and follow a broad grassy path through the bracken, aiming for the saddle between the two hills. (If the ground is wet underfoot, it may be preferable to keep to the tramway track.) Pass between two cairns (large piles of stones) between Weatherdon Hill and Butterdon Hill. Make for Hangershell Rock ahead (there is no proper path but a number of parallel cattle tracks) and pass to the right of the rock to head downhill towards the tramway, following a prehistoric stone row which comes in from the right.

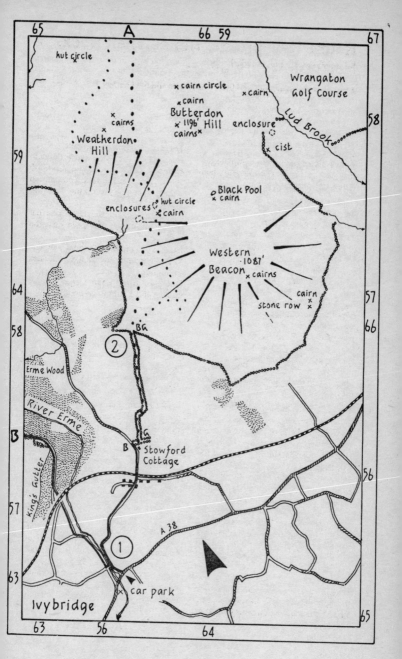

3 Follow the line of the stone row across the tramway (those who kept to the tramway should establish their position by glancing behind them until they can see Hangershell Rock with the stone row coming down the hill) and continue for about 200 yds. Now turn left (there is no proper path) and leave the stone row, aiming for the left flank of the hill with the low, flattened profile. The compass bearing is 262°. On reaching higher ground you will see on the skyline the *small* but prominent clump of trees known as Hanger Down Clump. Aim a little to the right of the Clump and you will arrive at a small car park with a gate in a stone wall giving access to a metalled lane. Follow this lane into Harford.

4 At the T-junction, riders should turn left and follow the road to Ivybridge, but walkers should turn right and walk past the church and over a bridge to reach Hall Farm on the right. Opposite Hall Farm is a footpath sign and a gate leading into an enclosed track which leads into a small triangular-shaped field. Follow the wall on the left to reach a gap in the wall ahead. Aim for the top left-hand corner of the next field and walk towards the wood. At the top of this field there is a gatepost in the wall. Pass through this and walk along the wall on the left which marks the boundary of the wood. About three quarters of the way across the field, turn left, through a gate with a footpath sign, into the wood and follow the clearly defined path to a hunting gate at the end of the wood. Bear slightly right and walk through the bracken along a well-defined path to a gate in a stone wall. Continue forward across two more fields, following the orange waymarks to reach an enclosed track.

5 Follow the track almost to the farm, then turn right to climb a ladder stile, follow the waymarks to another ladder stile and pass through the gate ahead which leads into an enclosed track. Follow this track, ignoring two enclosed tracks which run off to the right, until reaching Pithill Farm. Just before the farm, turn right along a roughly metalled lane which drops downhill to reach a railway viaduct. (See map on previous page.) Pass under the viaduct and fork left along the road all the way into Ivybridge (there is a pavement on the left-hand side).

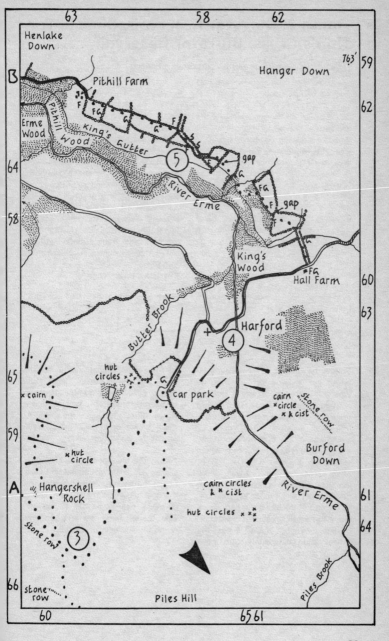

Henlake
Down

Hanger Down

763' 59

B

Pithill Farm

62

Erme
Wood

Pithill Wood

King's Gutter

F

FG

G

G

F

gap

64

5

G

FG

58

River Erme

F

gap

F

King's
Wood

FG

Hall Farm

60

63

Butter Brook

Harford

4

hut
circles

G

car park

65

cairn
× circle
× cist

Stone row

× cairn

59

× hut
circle

Burford
Down

A

Hangershell
Rock

River Erme

61

cairn circles
× cist

64

hut circles × × ×

stone row

3

66

stone
row

Piles Hill

60

6561

Piles Brook

Route 2. Burrator Reservoir, Sheeps Tor, Nun's Cross, Burrator Reservoir

A fairly demanding route mostly across open moorland

Distance: 8 miles
For: Walkers and riders
Terrain: Moderately difficult
Route-finding: Moderately difficult

Maps: 1:25000 sheets SX56, SX66/76, SX67, SX57; 1:50000 sheet 202; 1:63360 Tourist Map
Start: The car park at the eastern end of Burrator Reservoir near Norsworthy Bridge, grid reference SX568694
Parking: Plentiful at grid reference SX568694
Buses: Western National service 57 Plymouth to Burrator operates on Sundays and Bank Holidays during the summer. Alight at Norsworthy Bridge
Refreshments: None

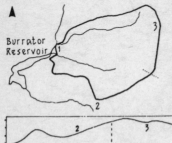

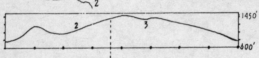

Follow the road round the reservoir for about ½ mile. Look for a clearing on your left with a track and a boulder with an orange waymark. Turn left up the track and where it turns sharp left, following a stone wall, continue ahead and shortly bear right to follow a path through the bracken which climbs up Sheeps Tor. On top of Sheeps Tor, turn left and walk down the steep slope to a clear path which runs parallel to the forest on your left. At the end of the forest the path drops down to a small stream not marked on Ordnance Survey maps. Cross the stream and immediately turn right to follow the stream, aiming for the small plantation ahead. There is no proper path, but a number of sheep tracks run through the bracken and it is not difficult to follow the route. At the fir plantation you will meet a track and at this point turn left.

Follow the track past some boundary stones which are not marked on Ordnance Survey maps until reaching the top of a hill where there is a crossing of tracks near some old enclosures. Take the left-hand fork and continue round the shoulder of the hill.

Continued on p. 42

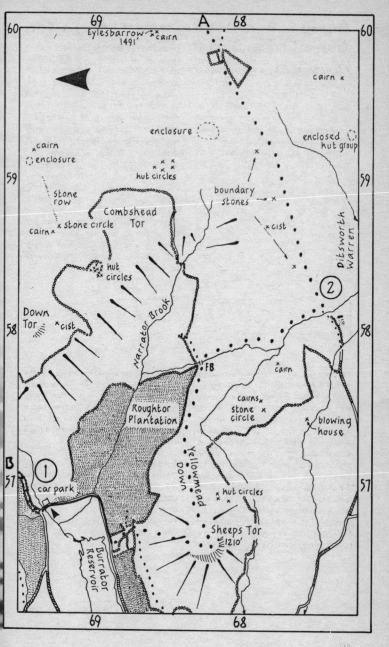

60
69
A
68
60

Eylesbarrow
1491'
×× cairn

cairn ×

enclosure

enclosed
hut group

×cairn
enclosure

× ×
× ×
hut circles

× ×
boundary
stones

59
59

stone
row

Combshead
Tor

× cist

cairn × × stone circle

Ditsworth Warren

hut
circles

×

Down
Tor × cist

58
Narrator Brook
58

FB

× cairn

Roughtor
Plantation

cairns×
stone ×
circle

× blowing
house

1
B
57
57

car park

Yellowmead
Down

× hut circles
× ×

Burrator Reservoir

Sheeps Tor
1210'

69
68

41

After about 200 yds, fork left and continue curving round the edge of the hill. Shortly afterwards another track comes in from the right. Continue down the hill on the clear track until reaching Nun's Cross Farm.

3   Keep to the left of the farm, past the cross, and continue forward up the hill until coming to the first *stony* track which crosses the path. Turn left and follow the stony path, which very soon becomes a wide but much less distinct grassy track that marches through the heather to curve round to the right to reach a very clear stony track at a T-junction. At this point turn left and follow the stony track for about 1½ miles over the Devonport Leat and past a cross to a fir plantation at a double gate. Pass through the gate and continue forward until reaching the reservoir near the car park.

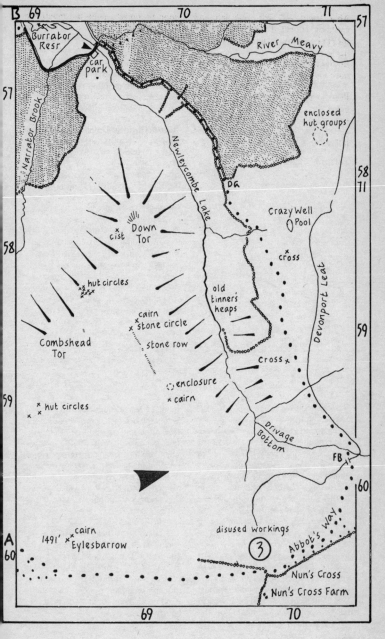

B 69 70 71

Burrator Resr

River Meavy

car park

Narrator Brook

enclosed hut groups

57

58
71

Newleycombe Lake

DA

Crazy Well Pool

Down Tor

cist

cross

hut circles

old tinners heaps

Devonport Leat

cairn
stone circle

stone row

Combshead Tor

Cross

59

enclosure
cairn

hut circles

Drivage Bottom

FB

60

disused workings

1491' cairn
Eylesbarrow

3

Abbot's Way

A
60

Nun's Cross

Nun's Cross Farm

69 70

Route 3. Princetown, Foggintor, Routrundle, South Hessary Tor, Princetown

A fairly strenuous walk which includes stretches of open moorland with no proper path as well as some well-defined tracks

Distance: 10 miles (but can be shortened to 8½ miles)
For: Walkers and riders
Terrain: Difficult

Burrator Reservoir

Route-finding: Difficult
Maps: 1 : 25000 sheet SX56, SX57, SX67; 1 : 50000 sheet 191; 1 : 63360 Tourist map
Start: Princetown, at the junction of the B3212 and B3357, grid reference SX590735
Parking: There is a large car park in Princetown
Buses: Western National service 82 Plymouth to Moretonhampstead operates on Saturdays, Sundays, Wednesdays and Bank Holidays during the summer. Service 613 Tavistock to Princetown, operated by J. R. Striplin, runs throughout the year from Mondays to Fridays
Refreshments: There are several cafés and public houses in Princetown

1 From Princetown take the B3212 road towards Yelverton. After passing the de-restricted sign there are two identical cottages on opposite sides of the road. Turn right down the far side of the right-hand cottage following a clear track which follows a stone wall and later a barbed-wire fence. On reaching the plantation, turn left and then immediately right, crossing the old railway track. Walk up the side of the plantation for about 20 yds and then turn left along a narrow but well-defined path which runs approximately parallel to the railway. The path gets less distinct when climbing Foggintor – if necessary follow a compass bearing of 271° and keep well to the left of the spoil heaps of the

quarry. If you have judged it right you will come out at a point where a track leaves the railway and goes right into the quarries. This can be further identified by a small concrete platform on the right-hand side and the remains of the chimney of a ruined building on the left-hand side. You will then see the bridleway running downhill towards a bridge.

The next part is tricky, for there is no very clear path. Look down the valley and about ½ mile ahead will be seen a rough track. Aim for this and make your own way through the rough pasture and boulders, and cross a stream. A compass bearing of 246° is about right. **2**

44

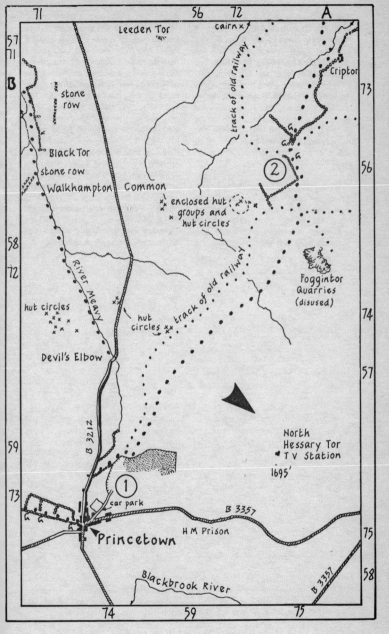

B

Leeden Tor

cairn ×

track of old railway

Criptor

stone row

Black Tor

stone row

Walkhampton Common

enclosed hut groups and hut circles

②

Fogginter Quarries (disused)

River Meavy

hut circles

hut circles

track of old railway

Devil's Elbow

B 3212

①

car park

North Hessary Tor T V Station

1695'

B 3357

Princetown

H M Prison

B 3357

Blackbrook River

Pass through a gate in a stone wall and continue forward, following a stony track. Soon a wall comes in from the right and there is a gate across the track you are following. Shortly before reaching the gate, turn left along another track with a wall on the right-hand side which becomes an enclosed track and runs past Routrundle, an abandoned farm. The track now crosses the open moor to reach the railway and then continues forward to reach a small car park on the main road.

3 The next part is not a right of way and no proper path exists. Cross the road and make for the forest ahead, keeping Sharpitor on your right. On reaching the forest turn right and follow the wall on your left until reaching the leat.

4 At the leat a choice has to be made. Those wanting a shortened route should turn left across the stile into the forest and follow the leat for about a mile to where it crosses the River Meavy by an aqueduct at the bottom of Raddick Hill. Now follow the right-hand bank of the Meavy to reach the road at the Devils Bridge. Turn right and follow the road to Princetown, walking on the grassy left-hand verge.

5 Those wanting a longer walk should turn right at the leat, follow the track for a few yards and then turn left down a sandy cart track which enters the forest. Follow the track to Leathertor Bridge and then turn right. This will bring you to a track at a T-junction. Turn left and follow this track which follows the forest edge to a gate.

Continued on p. 48

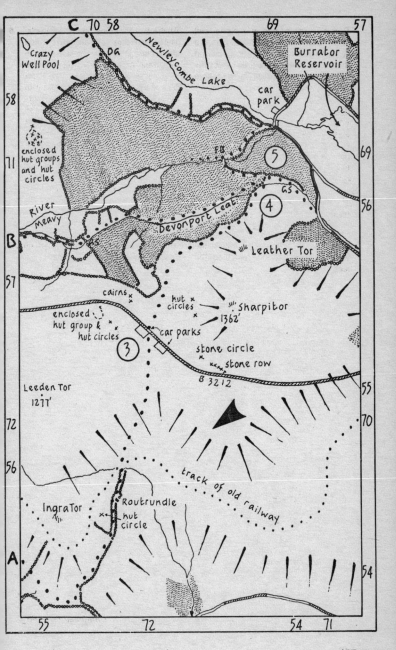

Continue across the open moor through some peat workings and two fords to reach a footbridge and the Devonport Leat. About 400 yds after the footbridge a track crosses at a boundary stone.

Turn left and follow the clear track past South Hessary Tor and into Princetown. **6**

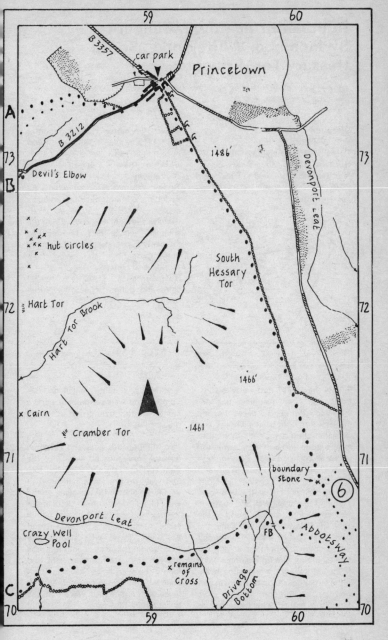

B 3357

car park

Princetown

B 3212

1486'

Devonport Leat

Devil's Elbow

x
x x
x x hut circles
x x x
x

South
Hessary
Tor

Hart Tor

Hart Tor Brook

1466'

·1461

x Cairn

Nʳ Cramber Tor

boundary
stone x

⑥

Devonport Leat

Crazy Well
Pool

FB

Abbotsway

x remains
of
Cross

Drivage
Bottom

59   60
73
B
72
71
C
70
59   60

Route 4. Princetown, Bullpark, Swincombe, Whiteworks, South Hessary Tor, Princetown

A fairly level walk across open moorland mostly following clear tracks (in some places no proper path exists)

Distance: 7½ miles
For: Walkers and riders
Terrain: Moderately difficult
Route-finding: Moderately difficult
Maps: 1:25000 sheets SX57 and SX67; 1:50000 sheet 191; 1:63360 Tourist Map

Start: Princetown at the junction of the B3212 and the B3357, grid reference SX590735
Parking: There is a large car park in Princetown
Buses: Western National service 82 Plymouth to Moretonhampstead operates on Saturdays, Sundays, Wednesdays and Bank Holidays during the summer. Service 613 Tavistock to Princetown, operated by J. R. Striplin, runs throughout the year from Mondays to Fridays
Refreshments: There are several cafés and public houses in Princetown

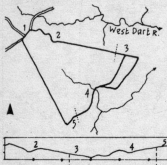

1   Follow the B3212 eastwards towards Postbridge until reaching the de-restricted sign. Forty paces beyond this sign turn right beside a house and pass through a gate. Walk forward to meet a stone wall and then bear left to follow an enclosed track. Pass through a gate on to the open moor and continue forward, keeping the stone wall on your right. Pass through some gateposts in a stone wall and continue forward, bearing slightly round to the right, still following the wall. Cross the Devonport Leat by a stone footbridge with a gate. Just before reaching the farm buildings, turn right along a well-defined stony track which soon bears to the left, drops down to a stream and then passes through some double gates in a barbed-wire fence before reaching a roughly metalled lane. Turn left and walk past a house and a stone barn to a gate giving access to the open moor.

Pass through this gate and continue   2
forward for about 50 yds until the track divides. Take the left-hand fork and walk up the slope parallel to a wire fence about 200 yds away on the left. Follow this straight track for about 2 miles until reaching a gate in a wire fence. At this point a decision has to be made. Those who doubt their route-finding abilities should not pass through the gate but turn right and follow the wire fence, keeping it on their left until reaching another wire fence with a gate in it. Note that this is not a right of way.

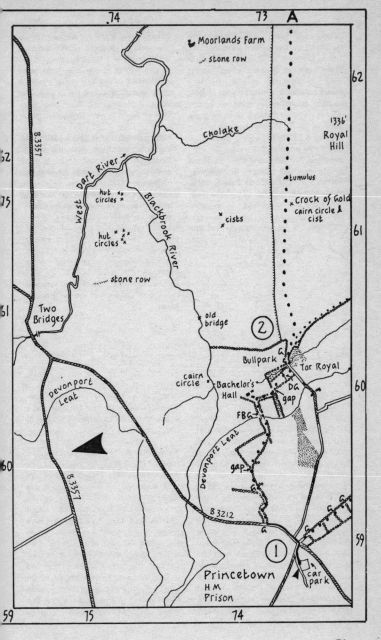

Moorlands farm
stone row

Cholake

B 3357

West Dart River

Blackbrook River

hut circles
hut circles

stone row

cists

1336'
Royal Hill

tumulus

Crock of Gold
cairn circle
cist

Two Bridges

old bridge

②

Bullpark

Tor Royal

cairn circle

Bachelor's Hall

Devonport Leat

DG
gap

FBG

gap

Devonport Leat

B 3357

B 3212

①

Princetown
H M Prison

car park

3 To follow the definitive route (which riders *must* use), pass through the gate and continue forward downhill. Some distance on the left is a stone wall. There is a gate in this wall about 300 yds from the gate in the wire fence through which you came. Exactly opposite this gate, turn right and you should be able to make out a sunken path. Follow this path following a compass bearing of 224°. If you have no compass, walk midway between the valley and the wire fence which you will glimpse occasionally on the right. There is no proper path, as the sunken path peters out after a time, but here and there will be found a sheep track going in roughly the right direction. On reaching a gate and stile in a wire fence, look down on Whiteworks. There is still no proper path, so aim well to the right of Whiteworks, where there is a fenced spring on the hillside. Pass down the right-hand side of the spring and cross a stretch of fen before reaching the stream. The wooden footbridge has been destroyed but it is easy to jump across.

4 Now turn left and follow a path, bearing uphill and away from the stream. Continue to a gate which leads to an enclosed grassy lane which brings you to the road at Whiteworks. Follow the road until it crosses the leat and then bears sharp right and makes for Princetown.

Continued on p. 54

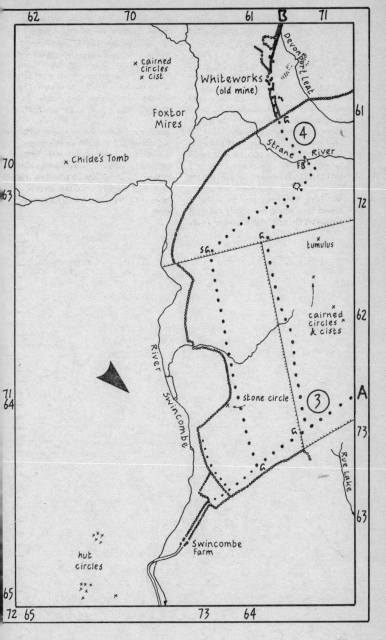

x Cairned
Circles
x cist

Foxtor
Mires

Whiteworks
(old mine)

Devonport Leat

x Childe's Tomb

Strane   River

FB

④

tumulus

SC

③

x
cairned
circles x
& cists

River

Swincombe

stone circle
x

A

Rue Lake

x x x
x

hut
circles

x x x
x x
x

Swincombe
Farm

62   70   61 B   71

70

63

71
64

65

72 65   73   64

61

72

62

73

63

5   Leave the road and continue forward along a grassy track. Ignore the first track which crosses and continue forward bearing slightly right. Just over the top of the ridge, in full view of Sharpitor and Burrator reservoir, a track crosses. Turn right and follow this very straight track past some boundary stones to South Hessary Tor and into Princetown.

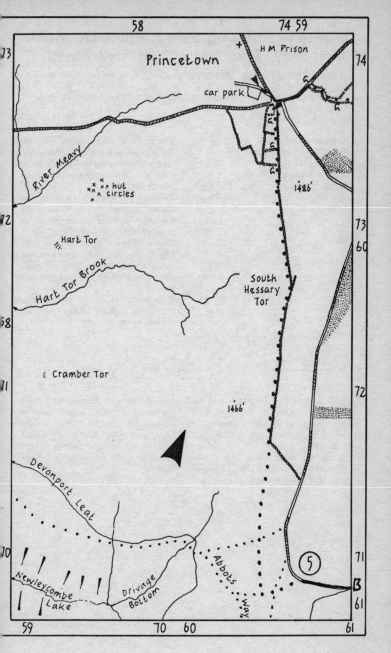

Princetown

HM Prison

car park

River Meavy

x x
x x x hut
x x x circles
x x

1486'

Hart Tor

Hart Tor Brook

South
Hessary
Tor

Cramber Tor

1466'

Devonport Leat

Newleycombe
Lake

Drivage
Bottom

Abbots Way

⑤

B

Route 5. Holming Beam, Black Dunghill, Lich Way, Traveller's Ford, Beardown Tor, Holming Beam

A tough and demanding walk across open moorland. *Check that the Merrivale firing range is open*

Distance: 10½ miles
For: Walkers and riders
Terrain: Difficult
Route-finding: Difficult
Maps: 1:25000 sheet SX57/67; 1:50000 sheet 191, 1:63360 Tourist Map

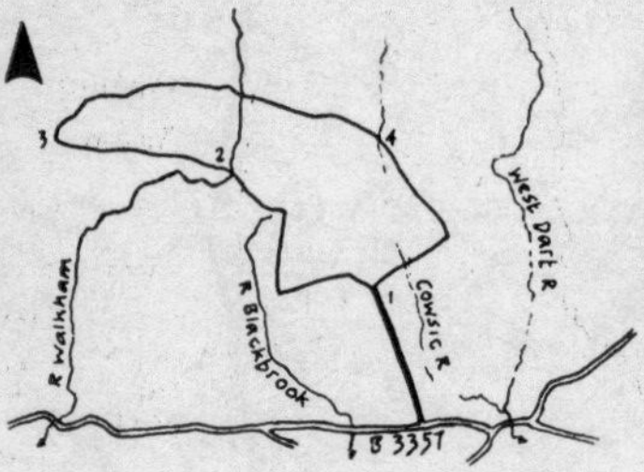

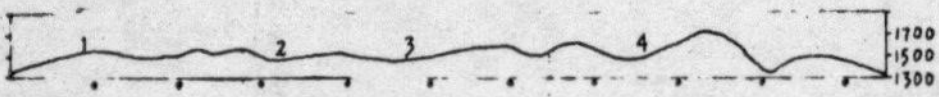

Start: From Two Bridges take the B3357 Tavistock road and after 1 mile take the first turning on the right along the military road which has plantations on the left.
Parking: There are several lay-bys on the military road. Park as far along the road and as close to the barrier as possible. Grid reference SX590769
Buses: Western National service 82 (the Transmoor Link). *This operates during the summer on Sundays, Wednesdays, Saturdays and Bank Holidays only*
Refreshments: At the Two Bridges Hotel, but walkers, unless residents, are not welcomed

1   Walk through the barrier following the wire fence on the left. Near the end of the fence, pass through a gate on the left and aim for a gate in the other fence. Pass through it, turn left and follow the fence for nearly a mile. About 50 yds before reaching a stream turn right along a holloway which was once a tramway. After about ¼ mile, the indistinct path bears left and crosses a boggy patch. You should now be walking towards the Prison Leat. Cross the Prison Leat by a footbridge and walk downhill to the River Walkham.

Continued on p. 58

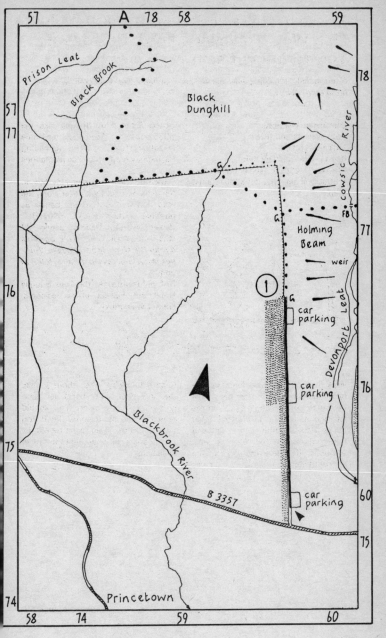

2 Cross the Walkham by the ford (if it is in flood it may be easier to cross a short distance upstream) and follow the clear stony track, which soon becomes much less distinct. Continue forward, aiming for White Tor ahead. When the whole of White Tor comes into view you will see, below it and a little to the right, a large standing stone towards which the path now runs.

3 On reaching the standing stone turn sharp right and follow the clearly defined path. This is known as the Lich Way (bodies were once taken along it for burial). Cross the Walkham at a ford and then the Prison Leat by a stone footbridge. Note that there are two bridges: it is important to cross by the upper bridge and then follow the more obvious track uphill.

Continued on p. 60

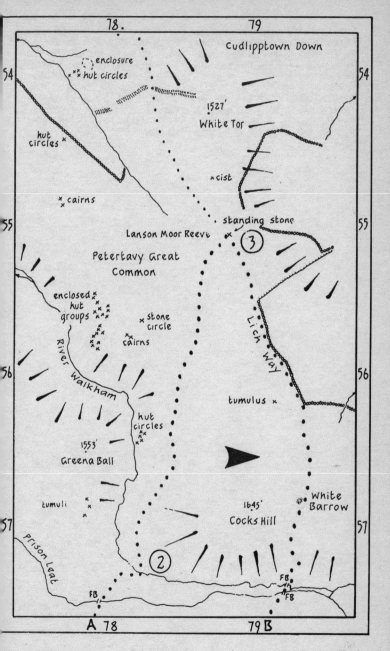

Cudlipptown Down

enclosure
hut circles

1527'
White Tor

hut
circles

×cist

cairns

standing stone

Lanson Moor Reeve ③

Petertavy Great
Common

enclosed
hut
groups

stone
circle

cairns

River Walkham

Lich Way

tumulus ×

hut
circles

1553'
Greena Ball

tumuli

②

1645'
Cocks Hill

White
Barrow

Prison Leat

FB

FB
FB

A 78

79 B

After a time the stony track peters out, but there is still a fairly clear path through the heather to the Cowsic River, which is crossed at Traveller's Ford.

4 Follow the clearly defined track uphill and, when the stone wall becomes visible, make for the gatepost. Make for Beardown Tor across the open moor (there is no proper path). At the top of the tor look down into the Cowsic valley on the right and you will see below the military track, which runs down to the river where there is a footbridge. Aim for the footbridge and then follow the track up the other side. Turn left at the top by the fence and walk back to your parking place.

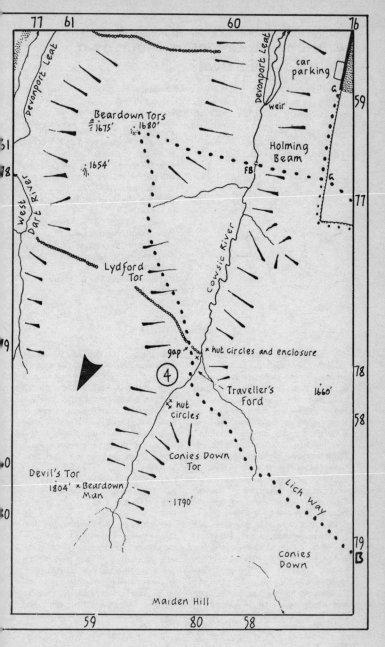

Route 6. Merrivale, around Cox Tor, Whitchurch Common, Moortown, Pew Tor, Merrivale

A walk mostly across open moorland but including some lanes

Distance: 7 miles
For: Walkers and riders
Terrain: Moderately difficult

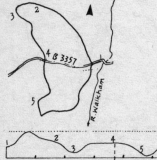

Route-finding: Moderately difficult
Maps: 1:25000 sheet SX57; 1:50000 sheet 191; 1:63360 Tourist Map
Start: The lay-by near the Dartmoor Inn on the B3357 east of Tavistock, grid reference SX550751
Parking: Plenty of parking at the start of the walk
Buses: Service 613 Tavistock to Princetown, operated by J. R. Striplin, runs from Mondays to Fridays throughout the year. Alight at the Dartmoor Inn
Refreshments: The Dartmoor Inn at the start of the walk

1 Walk up the hill past the Dartmoor Inn towards Tavistock. Just past the main entrance to the Merrivale quarry (that is, after passing the pair of quarry cottages and the single-storey building on the track to the main entrance) take a compass bearing of 346° and walk uphill across the open moor. In a few minutes you will come to the saddle between Middle Staple Tor and Great Staple Tor. (It is worth climbing to the top of Middle Staple Tor on the left for the magnificent views.) Continue forward, making for the small pool visible on the level ground below (not shown on any Ordnance Survey map). Bear slightly left round the massive bulk of Cox Tor and you will see Higher Godsworthy Farm below. Make for the metalled farm road and one field to the left of Higher Godsworthy Farm will be found a gate and a bridleway sign 'Bridlepath to Peter Tavy via The Combe'.

Pass through the gate and follow the 2 stone wall on the right. Cross a ruined wall and just past an outcrop of rock on the left, bear left and follow the turf and stone wall on the right. This will bring you to a gate giving access to an enclosed lane, which after a short distance opens out into a field. Follow the wall on the left and you will reach another gate and an enclosed lane. This, too, opens out into a field and by following the wall on the left you will come to a gate and bridleway sign at a metalled lane.

Turn left, walk past the farm and then 3 turn left along a metalled lane. Follow the lane until the metalling ends at the edge of the moor. Pass through the gate and follow the wall on your right. Where the wall turns right continue on up a wide grassy path to reach a metalled farm road. Turn right and follow the road to a point where the

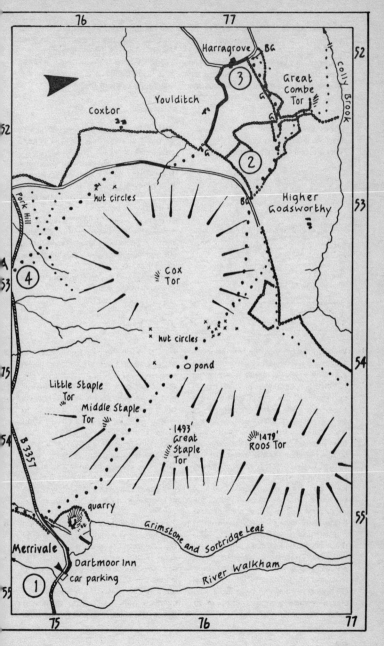

Harragrove BG

③

Great Combe Tor

Colly Brook

Youlditch

Coxtor

52

52

hut circles

BG

Park Hill

Higher Godsworthy

53

53

Cox Tor

④

53

hut circles

53

75

pond

hut circles

Little Staple Tor

Middle Staple Tor

·1493' Great Staple Tor

·1479' Roos Tor

54

54

54

B 3357

quarry

Grimstone and Sortridge Leat

55

Merrivale

Dartmoor Inn

River Walkham

①

car parking

55

55

75

76

77

highest visible point of Cox Tor on your left lines up with Coxtor Farm on your right. At this point search for a narrow but well-defined path which runs through the bracken on the left of the road. After about 200 yds the path becomes much wider – it is only the beginning of the path that is hard to find. Continue forward heading for Feather Tor on the skyline. The path contours Cox Tor and finally reaches the B3357 near a cattle grid which marks the edge of the moor.

Continued on p. 66

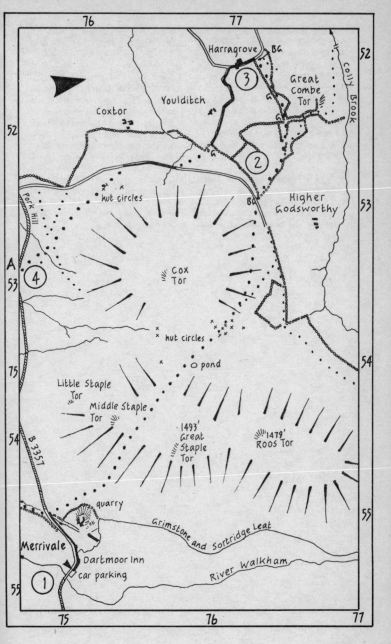

4 Cross the road and follow a broad grassy path which moves away from the wall on the right and then turns slightly right to follow the wall at a distance of about 200 yds. Cross a stream, drop down to the corner of the wall, turn right and keep the wall on your right. Cross another stream and continue forward, leaving the wall. After about 200 yds turn right down a grassy path towards some trees and on to the road.

5 Turn left and follow the road for about ¼ mile to a waste bin on the left about 50 yds before reaching Oakley Cottage, hidden among the trees on the right. At this point turn left, cross a footbridge and follow a track towards Pew Tor. Fork right and follow the grassy path to the base of Pew Tor and then, after climbing the tor to enjoy the view, walk round the right-hand side of the tor to follow a grassy path to reach a stony track which runs beside a stone wall. On reaching this track, turn left and follow it to a point where it becomes a grassy lane. Now leave the stone wall and drop down to the stream, heading for the corner of the wall ahead. On reaching it follow the grassy path alongside the stone wall all the way to the main road. On reaching the road, turn right and walk down the hill to the Dartmoor Inn.

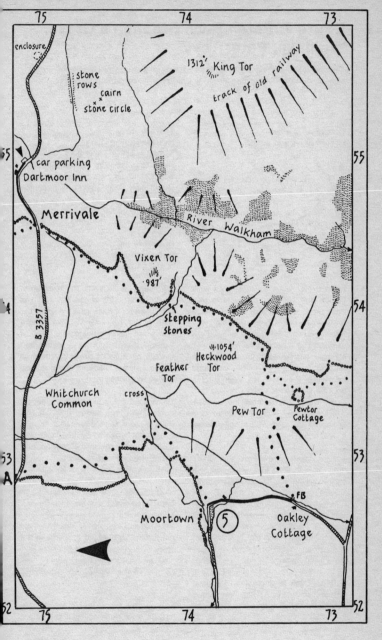

enclosure

stone
rows cairn
×
× stone circle

1312' King Tor

track of old railway

car parking
Dartmoor Inn

Merrivale

River Walkham

Vixen Tor

·987'

B 3357

Stepping
Stones

Heckwood
Tor ▲1054'

Feather
Tor

Whitchurch
Common

cross

Pew Tor

Pewtor
Cottage

FB

Moortown

⑤

Oakley
Cottage

Route 7. Peter Tavy, Stephen's Grave, Wedlake, Peter Tavy

A pleasant route along clearly defined tracks with a short stretch of open moor. After heavy rain the stepping stones at Wedlake may be difficult to cross

Distance: 5 miles
For: Walkers and riders

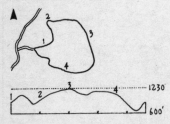

Terrain: Easy
Route-finding: Easy
Maps: 1:25000 sheet SX57; 1:50000 sheet 191; 1:63360 Tourist Map
Start: The car park below Smeardon Down near Peter Tavy, grid reference SX517778
Parking: The car park below Smeardon Down at grid reference SX517778
Buses: None
Refreshments: Peter Tavy has a public house

1   From the car park, turn left and walk up the hill. The lane deteriorates to a track and, at the top of the hill, a bridleway sign will be seen set well back on the left-hand side. Pass through the gate and follow the wall on your left to reach another gate at the end of the field. Continue following the wall on your left to another gate which gives access to a stony track. This almost immediately bears right and joins a metalled lane beyond a ford with a footbridge beside it.

2   Turn right along the lane and where the metalling ends fork left to follow a stone wall which 100 yds later gives access to a walled stony track. Follow this track to a gate at the end which leads on to the open moor. Pass through the gate and follow the wall on your right. After 300 yds the path is again enclosed for a short distance. On emerging on to the open moor again make for the stone wall ahead, noting the fine example of an enclosed hut group on your left below White Tor. Continue to follow the wall until it forms a corner, then, instead of

following it round to the right, continue straight ahead for 150 yds and make for a track which crosses the path at Stephen's Grave. (An upright unmarked stone indicates the grave of George Stephens, who committed suicide because of the unfaithfulness of his fiancée. Suicides could not be buried in consecrated ground.)

Cross the track and follow a pleasant 3 grassy path which after 500 yds follows a stone wall down to a stream. Cross the stream by the stepping stones, pass through the gate beyond it and you will find yourself in a rough pasture with a stone wall on your left with trees growing in it. (If the stepping stones cannot be crossed, go back to Stephen's Grave and turn left along the track which will take you into Peter Tavy.) Bear right and go diagonally up the field to a gate in the stone wall. Pass through the gate and turn right along a track which runs parallel to the wall on your right but about 100 yds beyond it.

Follow the track for about ½ mile 4 and on your right you will see a gate

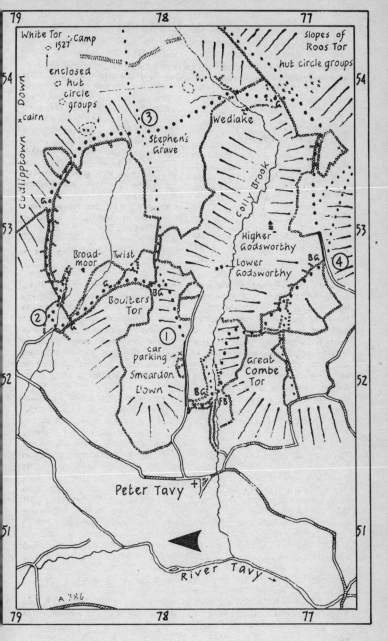

White Tor · Camp
∴ 1527

enclosed
hut
circle
groups

×cairn

Cudlipptown Down

Slopes of
Roos Tor

hut circle groups

③

Stephen's
Grave

Wedlake

Colly Brook

Higher
Godsworthy

Lower
Godsworthy

BG

④

Broad-
moor   Twist

②

Boulters
Tor

BG

①

car
parking

Smeardon
Down

Great
Combe
Tor

BG

FB

Peter Tavy ✝

River Tavy →

A 386

and bridleway signpost pointing towards Peter Tavy. Pass through the gate and follow the wall on your right until reaching a ruined wall which crosses the field. Pass through a gap in this wall, ignoring the gate on your right. Continue in the same direction, following the wall on your right, and after 150 yds pass through a gap in the wall ahead. Continue diagonally across the next field touching the irregularly shaped wall on your right at one point, and then pass through some gorse bushes to a gate at the bottom of the field which gives access to an enclosed lane. Continue down the lane until emerging at Great Combe Tor. Make your way down the very steep slope on the right-hand side of the tor and at the foot of the clitters turn left and follow the path which runs parallel to the stream but about 200 yds above it. This path passes a stone pond and crosses the stream by a footbridge. Immediately ahead will be seen a bridleway sign. Take the narrow enclosed path signposted 'To Smeardon Down' to reach the road. Turn right and walk to the car park.

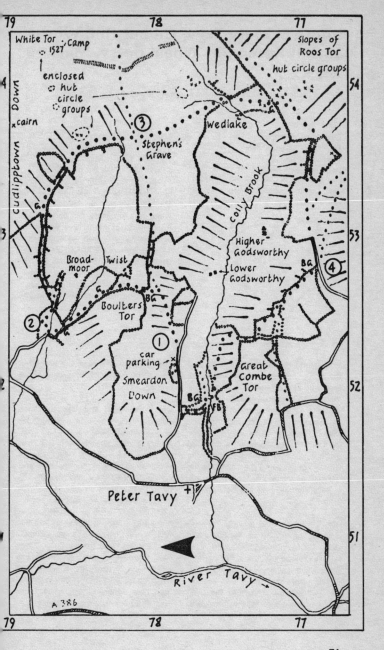

White Tor · Camp
☼ 1527

enclosed
hut
circle
groups

× cairn

Cudlipptown Down

Slopes of
Roos Tor

hut circle groups

③

Stephen's Grave

Wedlake

Colly Brook

Broad-
moor

Twist

G

Higher-
Godsworthy

Lower
Godsworthy

BG

④

Boulters
Tor

BG

②

①

car
parking

×

Smeardon
Down

Great
Combe
Tor

BG

FB

Peter Tavy

†

River Tavy

A 386

71

Route 8. Mary Tavy, Gibbet Hill, Wheal Jewell Reservoir, Wheal Betsy, Mary Tavy

A route across open moorland with an opportunity to see an old mine

Distance: 6 miles
For: Walkers and riders
Terrain: Easy
Route-finding: Easy

Maps: 1:25000 sheets SX48, SX58, SX47, SX57; 1:50000 sheet 191; 1:63360 Tourist Map
Start: Mary Tavy on the A386
Parking: Very difficult. It is sometimes possible to park near the War Memorial or by the council houses. There is a roadside car park on the A386 north of Mary Tavy where the path crosses the road (see paragraph 3), grid reference SX513822
Buses: Service 618 Tavistock to Okehampton, operated by C. J. Down, runs from Mondays to Saturdays
Refreshments: A public house and a café in Mary Tavy

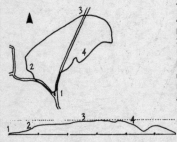

1   Walk along the lane which runs past the chapel opposite the war memorial, turn right at the T-junction and follow the road to the cattle grid. On the right of the road at the edge of the moor will be seen two paths. Ignore the one that follows the stone wall and take the one that runs parallel to the road for a little way and then contours Gibbet Hill, keeping the valley on the left. (Ordnance Survey maps show only a path running much closer to the road.)

2   About 500 yds after leaving the road is a junction of paths marked by a few stones. Fork right and head north. This path is crossed by others, but the line is clear and it scarcely varies in height. A mile or so after the pile of stones, you will see on your right the telegraph poles which follow the A386.

The path joins the road at a waste bin about 200 yds north of a small stone bridge.

Cross the A386 and take the track which leaves it at right-angles, crossing another track after 100 yds. Nearly ½ mile after leaving the road are some old workings which can be mistaken for a track. Ignore them and continue forward for another 100 yds or so to fork right along a clear track used by the army. Follow this track for ¼ mile, past various military structures and a large building on the left with a lifebuoy on the wall, to reach an enclosed lane. *Do not enter it* but turn sharp right and take the track which heads towards a wall. On reaching the wall follow it for 200 yds, then bear right through bushes, following a track to a gate in a wall.

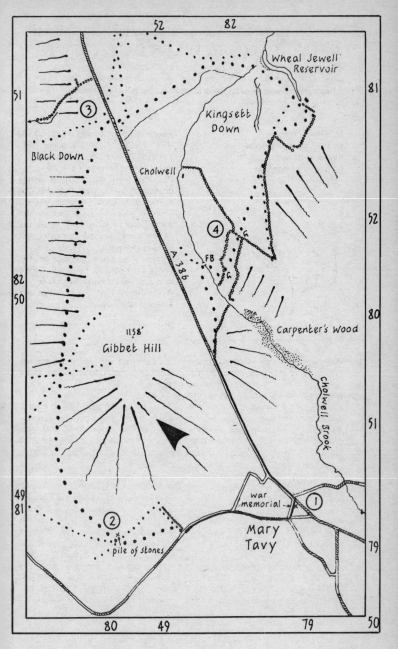

52 82

Wheal Jewell
Reservoir

51

Kingsett
Down

③

Black Down

Cholwell

④

52

A 386

FB

82
50

80

Carpenter's Wood

1158'
Gibbet Hill

51

Cholwell Brook

war
memorial

①

49
81

②

79

Mary
Tavy

pile of stones

50

80 49 79

4 Pass through the gate and continue down the track, moving slightly away from the hedge on the left to reach another gate. Pass through the gate, continue in the same direction for 100 yds, then turn sharp right to follow a stony track over a footbridge. On the right is Wheal Betsy mine, which was an important lead, silver and zinc mine. There is much evidence of mining activity. After crossing the bridge turn left and follow the rough road up the hillside to the A386. Turn left and drop down into Mary Tavy.

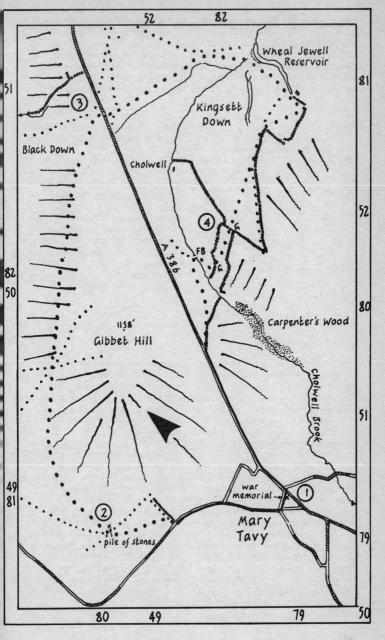

Wheal Jewell
Reservoir

Kingsett
Down

③

Black Down

Cholwell

④

G

A 386

FB

G

1158'
Gibbet Hill

Carpenter's Wood

Cholwell Brook

war
memorial → ①

②

Mary
Tavy

pile of stones

Route 9. Lydford, Dick's Well, King Wall, Lydford

A walk over open moorland following clearly defined tracks. *Check that the Willsworthy firing range is open*

Distance: 7 miles
For: Walkers and riders
Terrain: Moderately difficult
Route-finding: Moderately difficult

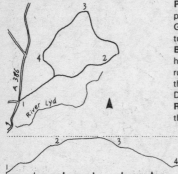

Maps: 1:25000 sheet SX48/58; 1:50000 sheet 191; 1:63360 Tourist Map
Start: The Lydford turn on the A386
Parking: There is a lay-by at a telephone box opposite the Moorside Garage on the A386 at the Lydford turn, grid reference SX523853
Buses: Service 618 Tavistock to Okehampton, operated by C. J. Down, runs from Monday to Saturday throughout the year. Alight at the Dartmoor Inn
Refreshments: A café in Lydford; the Dartmoor Inn at the start

1 Walk towards the Dartmoor Inn and, opposite the road junction, turn left along an enclosed track which emerges into a field at a gate. Inside the field the track divides. Take the left fork and follow the wall on your left to the river, where there is a ford, stepping stones and a footbridge. Look up the hillside. To the right is Brat Tor, with Widgery Cross on the top, and to the left is Arms Tor. Aim for the peat workings on the saddle midway between the two tors. There is a maze of paths, but once the top of the saddle is reached the path is clear.

2 Continue forward past the peat workings to a boundary stone at Dick's Well, a spring about 50 yds to the right of the path. Fork left 150 yds beyond the boundary stone to reach a range notice board, and fork sharply left. For 25 yds the path is indistinct but then joins another holloway. After about 300 yds, where the path forks, bear left to reach a stream at the ruin known as Bleak House. Beyond it, the path forks; bear left to reach an old tramway track on an embankment. Turn left and follow the tramway.

3 Immediately after crossing a stream, leave the tramway, turn left and follow a holloway parallel to the stream. After about ¼ mile you will reach the tramway track. Turn left and follow it to where it forks. Bear left (do not go on to the embankment) and where the embankment rejoins the main track fork right (do not go into the cutting). Follow this track to the fine stone wall, known as King Wall, and follow it to another wall where the track turns left 90°. Follow it to the river, where there is a ford.

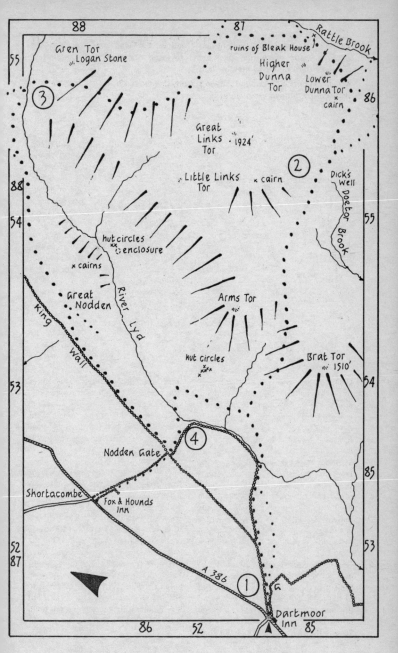

Gren Tor
"Logan Stone
③
88
87
Rattle Brook
55
ruins of Bleak House
Higher
Dunna
Tor
Lower
Dunna Tor
× cairn
86

Great
Links
Tor
"1924'
②
"Little Links
Tor
× cairn
Dick's
Well
54
88
Doctor
Brook
55
hut circles
×× enclosure
× cairns
Great
Nodden
River Lyd
Arms Tor
King
Wall
hut circles
×××
Brat Tor
"1510'
53
54
④
Nodden Gate
85
Shortacombe
Fox & Hounds
Inn
52
87
A 386
①
53
Dartmoor
Inn
86
52
85

4 Cross the ford and continue for about 50 yds up the hillside. Turn right and follow the path, which runs above the river bank to reach the footbridge, ford and stepping stones. Cross here and follow the wall and track to the enclosed lane leading to the starting point.

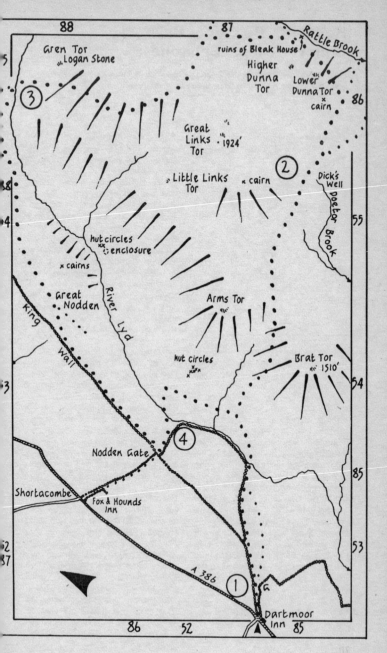

88

87

Rattle Brook

Gren Tor
"Logan Stone

ruins of Bleak House

Higher
Dunna
Tor

Lower
Dunna Tor
× cairn

86

③

Great
Links
Tor

" '1924'

②

Dick's
Well

Little Links
Tor

× cairn

Doctor Brook

55

hut circles
" enclosure

× cairns

Great
Nodden

River Lyd

Arms Tor

King Wall

hut circles
× × FA

Brat Tor
" '1510'

54

Nodden Gate

④

85

Shortacombe

Fox & Hounds
Inn

53

A 386

①

G

Dartmoor
Inn

86

52

85

Route 10. Belstone, Halstock, Cullever Steps, Belstone

A route along well-defined tracks and paths which includes a short stretch of open moor. *Check that the Okehampton firing range is open*

Distance: 5 miles
For: Walkers and riders
Terrain: Easy

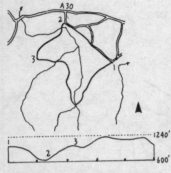

Route-finding: Easy
Maps: 1:25000 sheets SX59 and SX69; 1:50000 sheet 191; 1:63360 Tourist Map
Start: Belstone, south-east of Okehampton, grid reference SX620936
Parking: Very difficult
Buses: Service 625 Okehampton to Tordown, operated by Okeridge Motor Services, runs throughout the year Mondays to Fridays during term time. Western National Service 173 Newton Abbot to Okehampton operates Mondays to Saturdays (except Bank Holidays) during the summer months. Alight at the Belstone turn, a mile from the village
Refreshments: None

1 The route starts from the centre of Belstone. Follow the road towards Okehampton. Riders must keep to the road until reaching the railway bridge (see paragraph 3). Just beyond a cattle grid walkers should pass through a gate on the left-hand side of the road and make for a gap diagonally across the field. Pass through the gap and walk down the field, following the wall on your right, to reach a rudimentary stile at the bottom of the field. Cross the stile and follow the wall on your left to reach another stile which gives access to an enclosed lane with another stile beyond. Cross both stiles and you will find yourself in a field where a stile can be seen which gives access to the road after crossing a footbridge. At the road turn left and walk to the railway bridge.

2 Pass under the railway bridge and take the lane which goes off to the left on the other side of the bridge. At the bottom of the lane pass under the railway again and then cross the stream by the footbridge (riders will have to use the ford). Take the track which bears round to follow the general direction of the railway and when a wall becomes visible keep this on your right, taking care not to enter the field. In summer the branches of the trees hang low over the sunken track. At the end of the track is a gate.

3 The gate gives access to a road, where you should turn left. Walk up the road for about 200 yds and then turn along a gated, metalled farm road on your left. This will take you to Halstock, where you must pass through two gates at either end of the farmyard and then follow the stony track which goes up the hill to the right to reach a gate. Pass through the gate into the open moor and follow the wall on your left. When the wall turns 90°

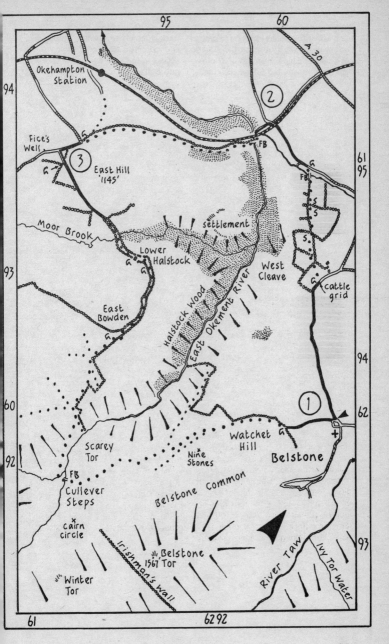

95　　60

A 30

Okehampton
Station

②

Fice's
Well

③　East Hill
'1145'

FB

61
95
FB
S
S

Moor Brook

settlement

S.

Lower
Halstock

West
Cleave

G

cattle
grid

93

East
Bowden

Halstock Wood

East Okement River

94

60

Scarey
Tor

Nine
Stones

Watchet
Hill

Belstone

①

62

92

FB
Cullever
Steps

Belstone Common

✶ cairn
circle

Belstone
1567 Tor

Irishman's wall

River Taw

Ivy Tor water

93

Winter
Tor

61　　　62 92

there is a junction of paths. Turn left and after 50 yds, at a junction of paths, continue forward to reach the stream at Cullever Steps. Bear left after crossing the stream and follow the clearly defined track. After about a mile a track goes off to the left. Ignore this, and continue to a gate which gives access to the road which will take you into Belstone.

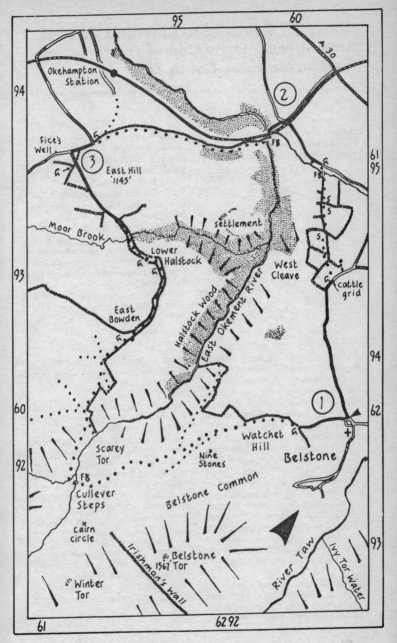

95   60

▲ 30

Okehampton
Station

② 94

FB

Fice's
Well

③ East Hill
'1145'

61
95

settlement

Moor Brook

Lower
Halstock

West
Cleave

93

cattle
grid

East
Bowden

Halstock Wood

East Okement River

94

60

① 62

Scarey Tor

Watchet
Hill

Belstone

92

Nine
Stones

FB

Cullever
Steps

Belstone Common

cairn
circle

Irishman's Wall

Belstone
1567 Tor

93

Winter
Tor

River Taw

Ivy Tor Water

61   62 92

Route 11. South Zeal, Cawsand Beacon, Small Brook, Little Hound Tor, Raybarrow Pool, South Zeal

A fairly demanding walk across open moor. *Check that the Okehampton firing range is open*

Distance: 6 miles
For: Walkers and riders
Terrain: Moderately difficult

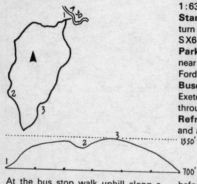

Route-finding: Moderately difficult (compass useful)
Maps: 1:25000 sheets SX69/79 and SX68/78; 1:50000 sheet 191; 1:63360 Tourist Map
Start: The bus stop at the South Zeal turn on the A30, grid reference SX648933
Parking: A small lay-by on the A30 near the National Benzole garage at Ford Cross. Grid reference SX648934
Buses: Western National service 383 Exeter to Okehampton operates daily throughout the year
Refreshments: Some public houses and a café in South Zeal

1 At the bus stop walk uphill along a metalled lane on the left-hand side of Newlyn Cottage. The metalling ceases just beyond Cawsand House and deteriorates into a rough track. Continue up the hill, always keeping to the widest track and following the signs to Crows Nest. On emerging on to the open moor, the rough sunken track continues ahead to reach a few sunken trees in a depression where there is a stream. Cross the stream by the stepping stones and continue forward until reaching the line of the disused leat. Follow this until it disappears, but by now the path is quite clear, running on the right-hand side of a wide depression. It will bring you down to the ford at Small Brook.

2 Do not cross the ford but turn left and take a compass bearing of 148°. Walk up the flank of the hill. On the saddle is a prehistoric stone circle. Just before reaching it, turn left along a sunken track which runs to the right of Little Hound Tor.

3 Where the path divides, bear right and keep to the right of Cawsand Beacon, following a clear path. On the right is the extensive fen known as Raybarrow Pool. On reaching a stone row, the path passes by the right-hand end, suddenly becomes less distinct and bears round to the right. Soon the path meets a stone wall, which should be kept on your right. The path now enters a steep enclosed lane with large boulders and a stream running down it. It soon joins another track, bears right and becomes a pleasant grassy lane. Pass through a gate and immediately bear left to reach the lane from which the walk started. Turn right and walk down the hill to South Zeal.

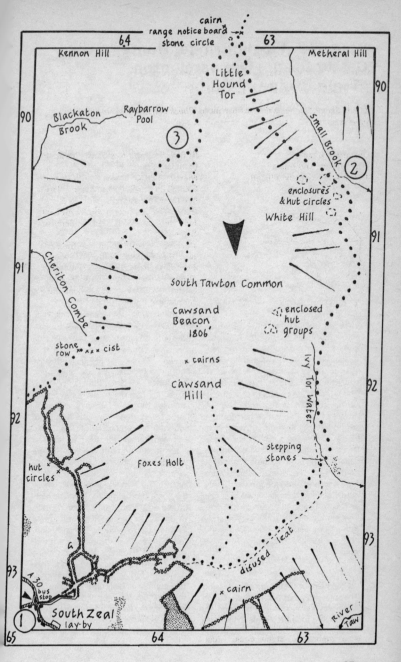

cairn
range notice board
stone circle

Kennon Hill   64   63   Metheral Hill

90   90

Little
Hound
Tor

Blackaton   Raybarrow
Brook   Pool

③

Small Brook

②

enclosures
& hut circles

White Hill

91   91

South Tawton Common

Cheriton Combe

Cawsand
Beacon
1806'

enclosed
hut
groups

x cairns

stone
row x x x cist

Cawsand
Hill

Ivy Tor Water

92   92

hut
circles

Foxes' Holt

stepping
stones

93   93

disused leat

A30
bus
stop

x cairn

River
Taw

①

South Zeal
lay-by

65   64   63

Route 12. Fingle Bridge, Hunter's Tor, Castle Drogo, Drewsteignton, Fingle Bridge

A very easy and beautiful walk through a gorge in the Upper Teign valley

Distance: 4½ miles
For: Walkers only
Route-finding: Easy
Terrain: Easy

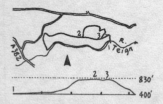

Maps: 1:25000 sheets SX68/78, SX69/; 1:50000 sheet 191; 1:63360 Tourist Map
Start: The car park, Fingle Bridge, near Drewsteignton, grid reference SX743899
Parking: At car park at Fingle Bridge, grid reference SX743899
Buses: Western National service 365 Exeter to Moretonhampstead operates Mondays to Saturdays throughout the year. Alight at Drewsteignton
Refreshments: Meals and snacks at the Angler's Rest, Fingle Bridge

1   From the car park at Fingle Bridge, recross the bridge and take the footpath opposite the Angler's Rest signposted 'County Road at Dogmarsh Bridge'. After about a mile there is a footpath sign near a footbridge over the river. Turn right and take the path signposted 'County Road at Castle Drogo and the Hunter's Path'. Pass a thatched cottage on the left and continue forward, still following the sign to 'The County Road'. At a gate, continue on up the metalled lane until reaching a signpost pointing to 'The Hunter's Path'. Turn right here and pass through the double gates into the National Trust grounds of Castle Drogo, high up on the left. The path suddenly turns very sharply left to run below Castle Drogo and above the valley from which you have come.

2   At the next footpath sign after passing the splendid viewpoint of Sharp Tor on the right, a choice has to be made. By continuing forward, Fingle Bridge will be reached in about a mile. To extend

the walk slightly, turn left and follow the footpath signposted 'Drewsteignton short cut'. (Those who take the shorter route to Fingle Bridge continue forward to the signpost mentioned in paragraph 3, p. 88.) Cross a stile on to a grassy path enclosed by gorse bushes and with a barbed-wire fence on the left and continue to another stile. Cross over and walk down the field to enter a wood at a hunting gate and a stile. Cross the stile and follow the path which runs very steeply downhill through woodland to the bottom of the hill, where there is a footpath sign. Take the path on the right signposted 'Hunter's Path to Road near Castle Drogo and Fingle Bridge'. On reaching a footpath sign, fork right and walk uphill to a left fork signposted 'Hunter's Path'. Continue to a fork on a very sharp bend. Take the right fork and, at a crossing of forestry tracks, bear right and continue forward. *Do not take the path on the right into the wood.* You will now come to the edge of the River Teign valley and are walking towards Castle Drogo.

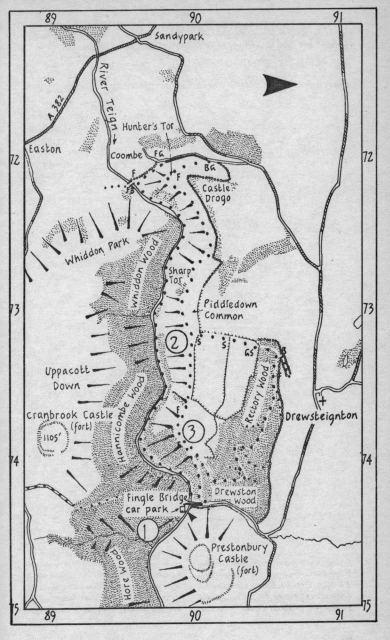

Sandypark

River Teign

A 382

Easton

Hunter's Tor

Coombe   Fa

F

Ba

Castle Drogo

Whiddon Park

Whiddon Wood

Sharp Tor

Piddledown Common

②   S   S   GS

Rectory Wood

Uppacott Down

Hannicombe Wood

Cranbrook Castle (fort)   1105'

F

③

Drewsteignton

Drewston Wood

Fingle Bridge car park

①

Hore Wood

Prestonbury Castle (fort)

72
73
74
75
89
90
91

3 At the footpath sign, take a very sharp turn to the left and drop down towards Fingle Bridge. Just above the Angler's Rest take the left fork to reach the road at a footpath sign. Turn right and walk down the road to the car park.

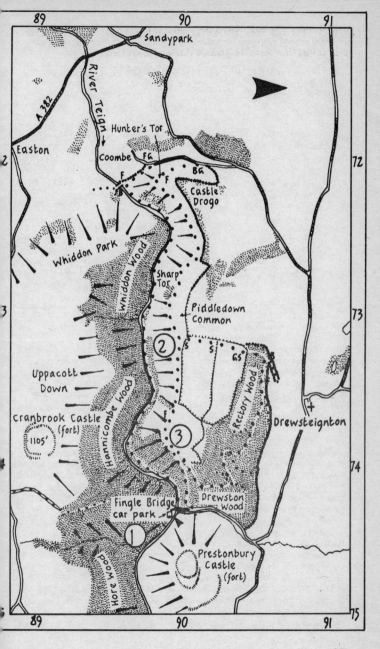

Route 13. Moretonhampstead, Butterdon Down, Willingstone Cottages, Cranbrook, Moretonhampstead

A walk along lanes and across fields

Distance: 4½ miles

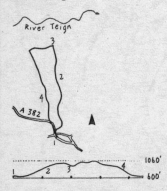

For: Walkers only
Terrain: Easy
Route-finding: Easy
Maps: 1:25000 sheet SX68/78; 1:50000 sheet 191; 1:63360 Tourist Map
Start: The centre of Moretonhampstead
Parking: Free public car park on the south-east (Bovey Tracey) side of the A382, grid reference SX755859
Buses: Western National service 365 Exeter to Moretonhampstead operates Monday to Saturday throughout the year
Refreshments: Plentiful in Moretonhampstead

1 Where the A382 Okehampton road turns sharp left, turn right at the Moreton House Hotel and immediately turn left into Lime Street. Follow this road to the bottom of the hill, where it crosses a stream. Turn left at the signpost 'Footpath to Road near Butterdon'. Pass through the gate and follow the clear path alongside the stream to a gap in a stone wall and continue forward until reaching a footbridge. Cross the footbridge and turn right to walk alongside the stream to a stile with a pond on the right and follow the stone wall bordering the stream to another stile. Bear left and walk diagonally up the hill to a way-marked stile and a footpath sign. Turn left and cross to a stile 20 yds ahead signposted 'Footpath to Road near Butterdon'. Cross the stile, turn right to keep the stone wall on your right and walk to the end of the field to a stile. Cross the stile, enter an enclosed path, cross another stile and turn right

to follow the wall on your right to a footpath sign at the wall on the other side of the field. (The Ordnance Survey map shows a slightly different route because the path was diverted in 1979.) Turn left at the footpath sign and follow the stone wall on your right to enter some woodland with a stream on the right. On reaching a gate, pass through it and continue uphill along an enclosed track. *Do not turn left off the track*. After passing Hill Farm Cottages on the left, the path meets the track which leads to the cottages. Turn right for a few yards and then left to follow the broad track to the road at a footpath sign.

2 Continue forward along the road until it turns sharp right. At this point turn left for 10 yds and then turn right to take the enclosed footpath signposted 'To Road near Willingstone Cottages'. After about 200 yds, turn right, enter the wood by a stile and hunting gate

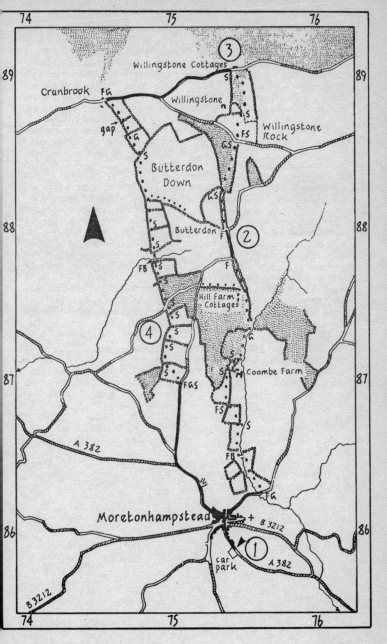

and follow a forest path to a gate and a stile at the road. Cross the road to another stile and follow the direction of the footpath sign which points towards a utility pole. Continue to the far corner of the field to a stile. Cross the stile and immediately turn left, and then right, to enter rough scrubland, and go downhill into woodland to reach a stile at the road opposite Willingstone Cottages.

3 Turn left and follow the road to a T-junction. Turn right, take the road signposted 'Chagford' and drop down the hill to Cranbrook. Turn left at a stone barn through a gate and stile signposted 'To Moreton via Butterdon Down'. Walk up the right-hand headland and pass through a gap in the stone wall. Continue forward to a gate and then to a stile at the top of the field which gives access to the open moor. Turn right and follow the stone wall on your right past a standing stone. On reaching a gate and a stile in the corner of two stone walls, cross the stile and follow the wall on your right. *Do not enter the enclosed lane.* Pass through a gap in a stone wall and continue forward down the hill, crossing two more stiles before reaching a causeway and stone footbridge which crosses a narrow marshy field. Cross the stile and continue forward up the hill, still keeping the wall on your right, to reach a wood. Enter the wood by crossing the stile and continue forward along the edge to reach the road.

4 Cross the road to a stone stile and walk up the hill along the edge of the wood, with a stone wall on your right. Cross another stile, continue forward to another stile and on to another and then another. Suddenly Moreton-hampstead is visible below. At this point bear left and walk diagonally across the field to a gate and stile at the road. Turn right and walk down the road to Moretonhampstead. Turn left at the main road, where there is a pavement.

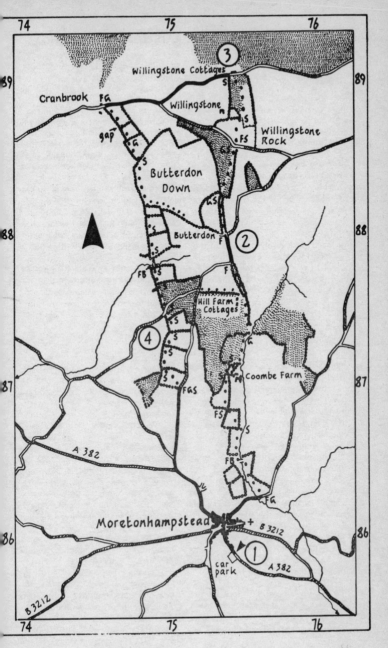

Willingstone Cottages

Cranbrook FG

gap

Willingstone

Willingstone
Rock

Butterdon
Down

Butterdon

Hill Farm
Cottages

Coombe Farm

A 382

Moretonhampstead

car
park

B 3212

A 382

B 3212

Route 14. Lustleigh, Lustleigh Cleave, Peck, Lustleigh

A very beautiful walk through a lovely wooded valley and nature reserve

Distance: 6½ miles
For: Walkers only
Terrain: Easy, but with some steep hills
Route-finding: Easy
Maps: 1:25000 sheet S X68/78; 1:50000 sheet 191; 1:63360 Tourist Map

Start: The war memorial in Lustleigh, grid reference S X786813. Lustleigh lies just off the A382, 2 miles north-west of Bovey Tracey
Parking: Difficult, as there is no car park. It is usually possible to find roadside parking in the village
Buses: Western National service 173 Newton Abbot to Okehampton operates Mondays to Saturdays in the summer
Refreshments: There are tea rooms and a public house in Lustleigh

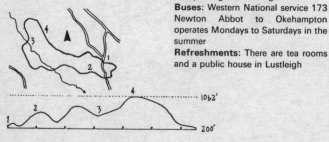

1 Stand at the war memorial with your back to the church. Walk down the metalled lane, keeping the Gospel Hall on your right, turn right and pass under the railway bridge. Turn right along a metalled lane signposted 'To Lustleigh Indirect' and continue until reaching a field gate. Walk down the left-hand headland and pass through a gate at the bottom of a field into the wood. Bear left to follow the stream, then cross the footbridge and follow the path which climbs the hill and passes under the railway to reach the road. Bear left, follow the road for 30 yds and then enter an enclosed track on the right. On reaching a road, turn left and walk to Rudge Cross. Turn right and follow the road signposted 'North Bovey'.

2 At the top of the hill, look for an enclosed track on the left signposted 'Bridlepath to the Cleave' (this is also the drive leading to Waye Cottage). Pass through a gate at the end of the track, bear slightly left and walk downhill to a junction of paths. Turn right, keeping a low stone wall on your left until reaching a signpost. Take the path signposted 'Bridlepath to Bovey Footbridge', bear left at the next fork and continue forward past a signpost to reach the River Bovey at a footbridge. Take the path signposted 'Public Bridleway to Water' and walk uphill, keeping a stone wall on your right, through the Bovey Valley National Nature Reserve. Follow the signposts until reaching a T-junction at a bridleway sign. Turn right and continue until reaching a roughly metalled track. Turn right and follow the track signposted 'To Manaton Indirect and Horsham for Lustleigh Cleave'. At the next junction of paths take the path signposted 'Horsham Steps'. Pass through some double gates and enter the farm garden, turn left by the front door and walk round the side

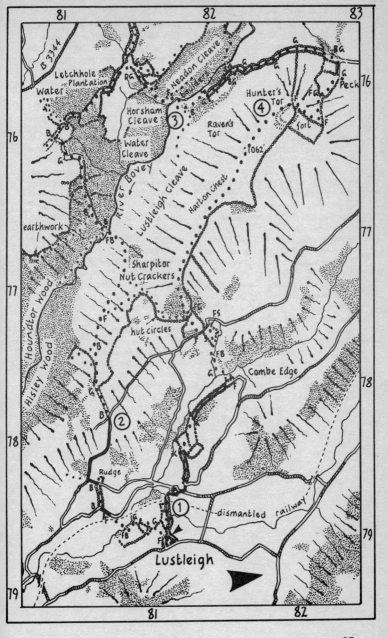

Lustleigh

of the house to reach two gates. Pass through the gate nearer the house, signposted 'Horsham Steps', and follow an enclosed path to a stile and down the hill to the stream.

3 Cross the stream by means of a massive pile of boulders (this is not as difficult as it looks at first) and bear left to follow the path which follows the general direction of the stream. At a signpost turn left and follow the path for Foxworthy to reach a gate at an enclosed lane. Continue forward, following this roughly metalled track through a farmyard and a number of gates until reaching a concrete road near Peck Farm. Turn right and follow the route signposted 'Bridlepath to Hammerslake for Lustleigh via Hunter's Tor and Sharpitor'. On reaching Peck Farm, pass through the waymarked gate on the right of the farm and walk up the left-hand headland alongside the farm buildings. At the top of the field, pass through a waymarked gate and continue forward, still keeping the wall on your left, and follow a sunken track. On reaching the top of this field, *do not pass through the stone wall*, but turn right at the footpath sign and keep the wall on your left to reach a gatepost in a stone wall near a footpath sign. At this point you are standing near an Iron Age hill fort dated about 500 B C. It is still possible to make out the general line of the ramparts.

There are a number of parallel paths. It 4 does not matter which one is followed as long as it keeps to the ridge and does not descend towards the valley, as they all converge at the point where the vegetation changes from open grassland to scrub and trees. The path then drops down steeply to the left to reach a gate and a signpost. Ignore the signposted path and continue forward downhill to reach a road. Turn left for about 30 yds and then turn right across a stile on a path signposted 'Footpath to Church Path for Lustleigh'. Drop steeply down to a stile and some awkward steps, cross another stile and immediately turn right to cross a stone footbridge to reach a gate which leads on to a metalled lane. Walk up the lane past the house and immediately turn right along a path signposted 'Lustleigh $\frac{1}{2}$ mile'. Pass through the remains of a kissing gate and immediately bear right around a boulder but *do not pass through the iron kissing gate into the field*. Follow the narrow path to another kissing gate and out into more open country. Cross the field and pass through a gap in the wall, ignoring the signpost, and continue forward, skirting some boulders on the left, to reach a kissing gate on the left-hand side of the house and an enclosed lane which emerges into a road. Turn right and almost immediately right again, and walk down to the church.

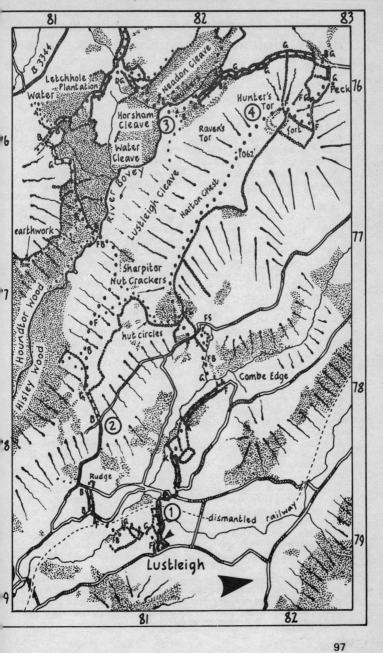

B 3344

Letchhole
Plantation
Water

Neadon Cleave

DG

Peck

Hunter's
Tor

④

Horsham
Cleave

③

Raven's
Tor

fort

F

Water
Cleave

FG

1062

earthwork

River Bovey

Lustleigh Cleave

Harton Chest

FB

Sharpitor
Nut Crackers

Hisley Wood

Houndtor Wood

F

FS

B

hut circles

FB

②

G

Combe Edge

B

Rudge

F

B

B

G

F

①

dismantled railway

FB

F

Lustleigh

97

Route 15. Haytor Rocks, Smallacombe Rocks, Hound Tor, Leighon, Haytor Vale, Bag Tor, Haytor Rocks

A somewhat demanding walk with some steep climbs

Distance: 8 miles

For: Walkers and riders. (Riders will have to divert slightly from the route and follow the road to Haytor Vale)

Terrain: Moderately difficult

Route-finding: Easy

Maps: 1:25000 sheet SX77; 1:50000 sheet 191; 1:63360 Tourist Map

Start: Haytor Rocks on an unclassified road 4 miles west of Bovey Tracey, grid reference SX760767

Parking: There is a large car park at Haytor Rocks, grid reference SX760768

Buses: National Park Pony Express service 891 Bovey Tracey to Widecombe operates daily throughout the summer. Western National service 193 Newton Abbot to Haytor operates Monday to Saturday throughout the year. Walkers who use this service should start their walk at Haytor Vale (paragraph 4)

Refreshments: The Rock Inn, Haytor Vale, serves excellent bar snacks

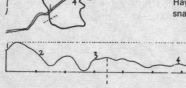

1 From the car park walk up the Haytor Rocks and admire the view. Walk across broken ground to Smallacombe Rocks (not very obvious from this viewpoint). If you have a compass, head due north. Smallacombe Rocks can be identified by aiming for the wood with a house below it on the hill on the other side of the valley. Walk towards this house and Smallacombe Rocks will become visible as you approach. There is no path until after crossing the old tramway, when one becomes visible running up to the rocks. Stand on the rocks and look down the valley. Below you in the wood is a house with a narrow path running through the bracken towards it. Follow this path, which about halfway down the hillside bears left and drops down much more steeply. At a clearing in the bracken, immediately before some stunted trees on the edge of the wood, a short cut to Leighon can be made. Look for a well-defined narrow path, difficult to find in the bracken, which runs off to the right 20 yds before reaching the stunted trees. Once found, the path is easy to follow through the bracken. It follows a wall alongside the wood and finally reaches an enclosed lane which, after

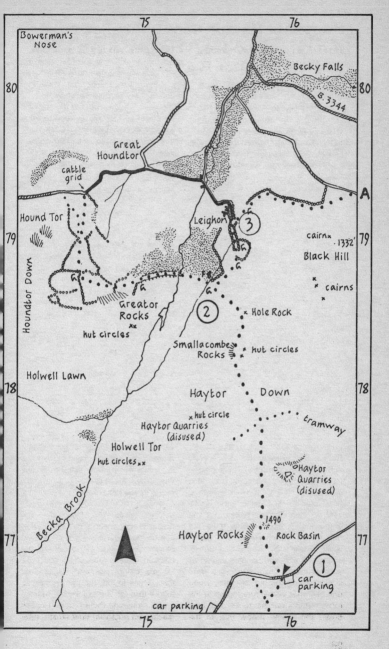

Bowerman's Nose

Becky Falls

B.3344

75

76

80

80

Great Houndtor

cattle grid

Hound Tor

A

Leighon

3

Houndtor Down

79

cairn

1332'

Black Hill

79

Greator Rocks

cairns

hut circles

2

Hole Rock

Smallacombe Rocks

hut circles

Holwell Lawn

Haytor

Down

78

tramway

78

hut circle

Haytor Quarries (disused)

Holwell Tor

Haytor Quarries (disused)

hut circles

Becka Brook

1490'

77

Haytor Rocks

Rock Basin

77

1

car parking

car parking

75

76

passing through two gates, will bring the walker to a junction of tracks near a large house near Leighon. Now turn to paragraph 3.

2 Those walking the whole route continue downhill to a gate and cross the stream by a stone footbridge. Go on up the hill, through a gate halfway up, to a gate at the very top next to Greator. Continue forward for about 300 yds, pass through some old enclosures and ruined buildings (the remains of a medieval village) then turn sharp right below Hound Tor to follow a clear path. Where this path forks, bear right to arrive at the road near a cattle grid. Turn right and walk down the steep hill. At the bottom is a road junction. Take the 'No Through Road' signposted 'Leighon' and at the end of it turn right and follow the road to the tiny hamlet of Leighon. Continue uphill and when the metalling stops follow the track to a T-junction with a sign 'Bridlepath to Becky Falls'.

Continued on p. 102

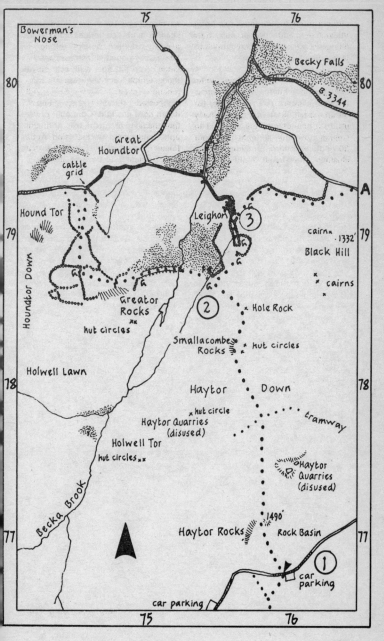

Bowerman's Nose

Becky Falls

B. 3344

Great Houndtor

cattle grid

Hound Tor

Leighon

③

cairn× ·1332'

Black Hill

× cairns

Greator Rocks

hut circles ×

② × Hole Rock

Smallacombe Rocks × hut circles

Holwell Lawn

Haytor   Down

× hut circle

Haytor Quarries (disused)

Holwell Tor

hut circles ××

tramway

Haytor Quarries (disused)

1490'

Haytor Rocks   Rock Basin

car parking ①

car parking

3 This is where the short cut rejoins the main route. Turn left and follow the sunken track, passing through a gate after about 100 yds, and follow the track to the road. Turn right and follow the road past North Lodge and up the hill. Look for a large wooden garage on your left and, 100 yds beyond it, a bridleway sign. Leave the road at this point, turn left and follow the path which runs alongside the wall. On reaching a disued quarry on the right continue forward for 100 yds to a junction of tracks opposite a gate. Fork right and follow a track which contours the hill above the road. When the track joins the road, turn right and walk uphill to a road junction. Follow the road signposted 'Haytor and Widecombe' and after about 100 yds follow the driveway to the Bel Alp Hotel. (At this point riders must continue along the road for ¾ mile and then turn left and follow the road into Haytor Vale. Riders rejoin the route at paragraph 4.) After passing a cattle grid you will see a footpath sign on the right-hand side.

After passing the hotel the metalling ceases and deteriorates to a track. Follow the track, passing through an unusual wooden turnstile to reach a road. Turn left and walk into Haytor Vale, which has a very pleasant inn.

4 Walk through Haytor Vale until reaching a road junction. Continue forward in the direction of Ilsington until reaching another road junction. At this point, turn right and follow a track signposted 'Bridlepath to the Moor'. Cross a stream and walk up the hill to a gate which gives access to the open moor. Turn left along the track which at first follows the wall on the left and then strikes out across the moor to reach the wall again near the top of the ridge. Bear right and then turn sharp right along a track which crosses. Follow this track all the way to the car park. Note that the car park which is visible for most of the way is not the Haytor Rocks car park but the one at Saddle Tor.

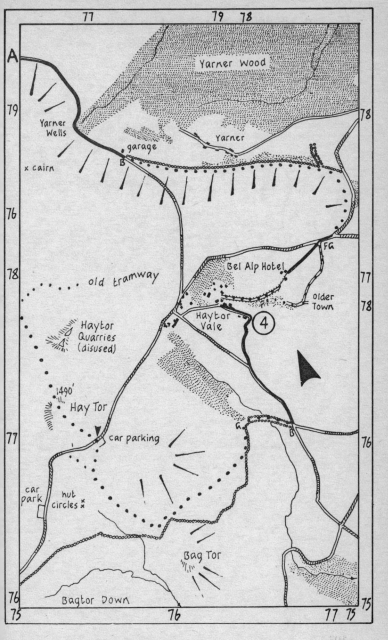

A

77   79   78

Yarner Wood

79

Yarner Wells

x cairn

garage

B

Yarner

78

76

old tramway

Bel Alp Hotel

FG

77

78

Haytor Quarries (disused)

Haytor Vale

Older Town

78

④

1490'

Hay Tor

77

car parking

76

car park

hut circles x x

B

Bag Tor

76

Bagtor Down

75

75   76   77   75

Route 16. Widecombe, Hameldown, Natsworthy, Bonehill Rocks, Widecombe

A demanding walk with extensive views

Distance: 7 miles
For: Walkers and riders

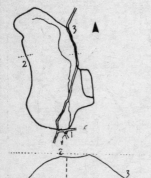

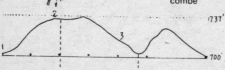

Terrain: Moderately difficult
Route-finding: Easy
Maps: 1:25000 sheets SX77 and SX68/78; 1:50000 sheet 191; 1:63360 Tourist Map
Start: Widecombe-in-the-Moor, grid reference SX719769
Parking: There are two public car parks in Widecombe
Buses: National Park Pony Express Services 891 Bovey Tracey to Widecombe and 892 Buckfastleigh to Postbridge operate daily throughout the summer
Refreshments: Plentiful in Widecombe

1 From the green in front of the church tower, take the road signposted 'Natsworthy'. Take the first turning on the left ('No Through Road' sign). This road climbs very steeply and then becomes a rough track. On reaching the open moor at a gate, continue forward and follow a grassy track which runs parallel to the wall on the right.

At the top of the hill a stone wall comes in from the right and a track comes in from the left. At this point, bear right and follow the wall on your right. Where the wall turns sharp right a track goes down beside it and another goes off at an angle. Continue forward aiming for the top of the hill ahead.

Continued on p 106

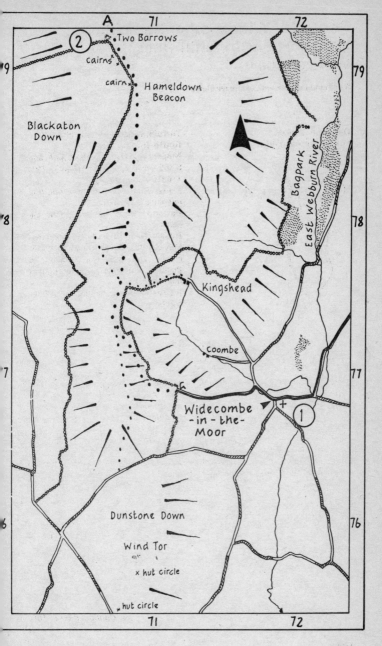

A 71 72

Two Barrows

cairns

cairn Hameldown
Beacon

Blackaton
Down

Bagpark

East Webburn River

Kingshead

Coombe

Widecombe
-in-the-
Moor

Dunstone Down

Wind Tor

x hut circle

x hut circle

79

78

77

76

71 72

2 At the top of Hameldown Beacon is a substantial barrow surmounted by a stone with 'Hamilton Beacon' carved on it. Continue forward along a broad track, keeping the stone wall on your left, for a short distance and then cross the open moor towards the barrow on the skyline. At Broad Barrow, where the path forks, take the left-hand track towards Hameldown Tor on the skyline. On the left is the remains of Hameldown Cross. On reaching Hameldown Tor, which has a trig point and a large cairn, take the path which runs off to the right and passes the R A F Stone, which records the death of some airmen in a crash in 1941. Here the path bears slightly left. Follow the broadest track until it is crossed by another track and at this point turn right. At the bottom of the hill, by three trees, on the right will be seen the walled prehistoric enclosure of Berry Pound on the hillside. The path drops down to follow the forest edge.

3 On reaching the road at a double gate and bridleway sign, turn right and walk down the road passing Isaford Farm on the right.

Continued on p. 108

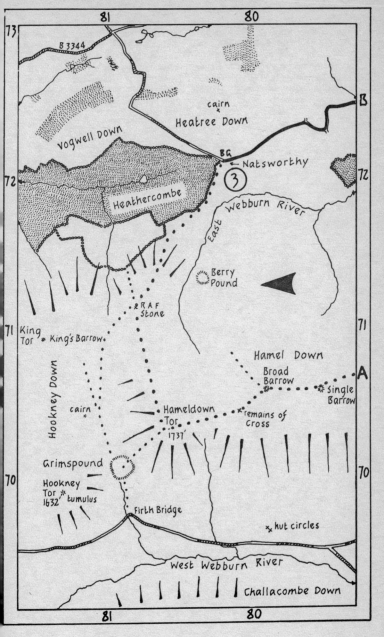

Cross a cattle grid in the road and immediately turn left to climb up a rough stony track. Pass through a gate on to the open moor and continue forward under the shadow of Honeybag Tor, following the wall on your right. (Energetic walkers can climb the narrow path to the top of Honeybag Tor, turn right and cross Chinkwell Tor and Bell Tor to reach the road at Bonehill Rocks.) On reaching the road at Bonehill Rocks, turn right and walk towards Widecombe (for most of the way there is a verge from which to escape the traffic). At the T-junction turn right and walk into the village.

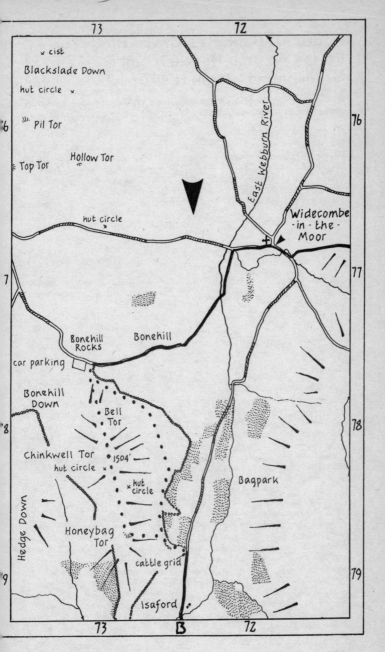

x cist

Blackslade Down

hut circle x

Pil Tor

Top Tor   Hollow Tor

East Webburn River

hut circle
x

Widecombe
- in - the -
Moor

Bonehill
Rocks   Bonehill

car parking

Bonehill
Down

Bell
Tor

Chinkwell Tor • 1504'
hut circle x

hut
circle

Bagpark

Hedge Down

Honeybag
Tor

cattle grid

Isaford

Route 17. Bennett's Cross, Birch Tor, West Coombe, Heathercombe, Grimspound, Bennett's Cross

A walk across open moorland and through forest and fields. There are some steep climbs and splendid views

Distance: 8 miles
For: Walkers only
Terrain: Moderately difficult
Route-finding: Moderately difficult
Maps: 1:25000 sheet SX68/78; 1:50000 sheet 191; 1:63360 Tourist Map

Start: Bennett's Cross car park on the B3212 ½ mile north-east of the Warren House Inn between Moretonhampstead and Postbridge, grid reference SX680818
Parking: There is a small car park at Bennett's Cross
Buses: Western National service 82 Plymouth to Moretonhampstead operates on Saturdays, Sundays, Wednesdays and Bank Holidays during the summer
Refreshments: Snacks are available at the Warren House Inn near the start of the walk

1 From the car park follow the clear track which runs up to Birch Tor, passing a walled enclosure. (The route shown on all Ordnance Survey maps does not exist.) At the top of Birch Tor, turn left and follow the clear path along the ridge until reaching a small roofless turf and stone construction. Turn right and follow a narrow path through the heather which climbs to the top of the ridge and then drops down to the road. On reaching the road cross over near a stone wall and continue forward uphill along a narrow path, keeping about 200 yds from the stone wall on the right. Just as the wall ahead comes into view, the narrow path forks. Take the left-hand fork and walk towards the wall, where you will find a gate in a kink in the wall. Pass through the gate, bear slightly left and walk downhill along a grassy path towards a pool. There are

some fine hut circles on either side of the path. Fork right towards the pool and pass through a stone wall at a gatepost. The path then drops down, follows a stream and passes a partly concreted access road which leads to the house on the left. Continue forward until reaching a gate giving access to a roughly metalled road at West Coombe Farm.

At the end of the first house on the **2** right the footpath to Natsworthy leaves the road beside a building which looks as though it may once have been an old chapel. Cross the stream by some stepping stones with orange waymarks and a stone step stile. Now bear slightly left and walk downhill towards a solitary stone in the middle of the field and make for a gatepost. Continue forward to the gate ahead on the other side of

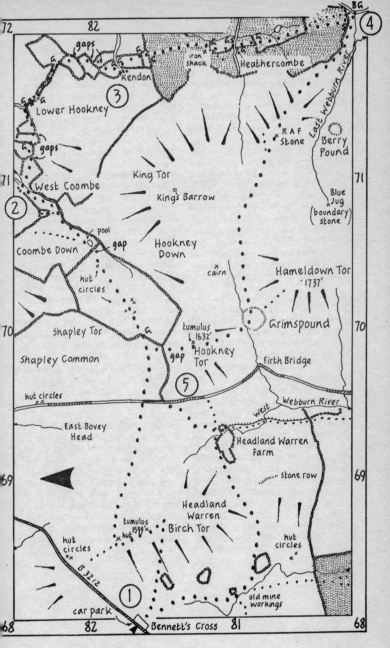

72 82

gaps
a
Kendon

3
Lower Hookney

gaps
b

71
West Coombe

2

pool
gap
Coombe Down

hut
circles

70
Shapley Tor

Shapley Common

hut circles
xx

East Bovey
Head

69

hut
circles
xx
B 32.12

car park

1

68 82

iron
shack
Heathercombe

BG

4

East Webburn River

RAF
Stone
Berry
Pound

King Tor
King's Barrow

71

Blue
Jug
(boundary)
stone

Hookney
Down

cairn
x

Hameldown Tor
1737

a
G

tumulus
1632
x
Hookney
Tor

gap

5

Grimspound

70

Firth Bridge

Webburn River
west

Headland Warren
Farm

stone row

69

Headland
Warren
Birch Tor

tumulus
1599 x
hut
x

hut
circles
xx

old mine
workings

68

Bennett's Cross
81

68

111

the field, cross a stream and walk diagonally to the other side of the field to a gatepost. Ignore the gate ahead and follow the embankment against the hedge on the right and you will come to a gate just before the house. This brings you into an enclosed lane. After 100 yds, turn right at a white house and walk to a gate which gives access to a farmyard. Pass through the farmyard, turning right past the farmhouse and then left through another gate which gives access to an enclosed track. Follow the track for the whole of its length until it emerges at a gate into a marshy field. Turn right and make for the gate about 50 yds ahead and then aim for the left-hand corner of the field where there is a ford. Cross the ford and aim for the left-hand side of the house opposite, where there is a gate which leads into a lane.

3 Cross the lane and enter another gate, walk diagonally across the field to a gate and cross to the forest ahead, where there is another gate. Continue forward following a pleasant forest path. After ¼ mile the forest clears and there is a crossing of tracks with an iron shack on the right. Turn left and go down to the gate and across the field, keeping the forest on your right, to a stile and a gate at Heathercombe. Cross the metalled bridleway signposted 'Natsworthy Gate for Widecombe Road' and pass through the gate on the left-hand side of South Heathercombe. Cross the field and make for the gate ahead which leads into the forest. Continue forward along the forest path, cross over a broad track and continue forward along a broad track. About 100 yds later, the track forks. Take the left-hand fork along the more obvious

track. In another 200 yds, pass a stone gatepost on your left, and then 25 yds later look for an inconspicuous path on the right, waymarked with orange splashes. Turn right into the forest to reach a gate and stile beyond which is the open moor. Cross the stile, turn left and follow the wall to a gate and a signpost at a road.

Turn right and follow the path sign- **4** posted 'Bridlepath to County Road near Grimspound'. Cross the stream at a ford and walk parallel to the stone wall on the edge of the forest. Where the wall bears round to the right, continue forward, passing three small trees, and then bear left and follow the main path up the hill, moving away from the forest. At this point there are a number of broad parallel paths, but you cannot go wrong providing you do not walk towards the forest, as all the paths merge further up the hill. On reaching a crossing of paths with a standing stone on your left, continue forward and follow a clear path all the way to the fascinating prehistoric settlement at Grimspound. Turn right and follow the clear path to the top of Hookney Tor and on to the gap in the stone wall ahead. Pass through the wall and turn left to reach the road.

Turn left and walk down the road for **5** a few yards and then turn right on a clear track which runs to the right of Headland Warren Farm. Follow the track and the telephone poles through some old mine workings, until reaching a major crossing of tracks in a valley. Turn right and walk up the hill towards the car park. There is no one obvious path but several parallel routes which all arrive at the road.

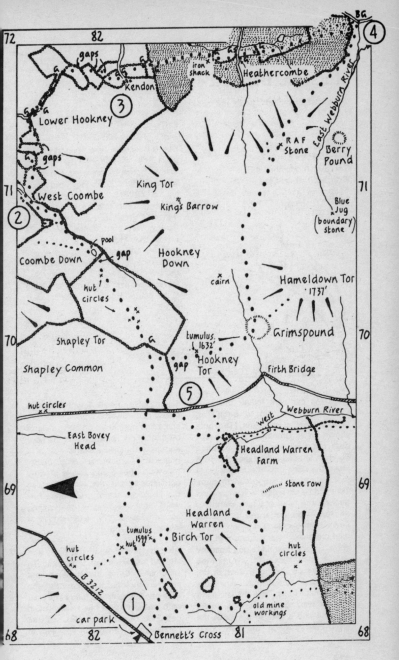

BG

72 82 4

gaps

iron shack

Heathercombe

Kendon

3

Lower Hookney

RAF Stone

East Webburn River

Berry Pound

gaps

71 71

West Coombe

King Tor

Blue Jug (boundary stone)

2

King's Barrow

pool

gap

Coombe Down

Hookney Down

cairn

Hameldown Tor ·1737'

hut circles

Grimspound

70 70

Shapley Tor

tumulus 1632'

Shapley Common

gap

Hookney Tor

Firth Bridge

5

hut circles

West

Webburn River

East Bovey Head

Headland Warren Farm

stone row

69 69

Headland Warren

Birch Tor

hut circles

tumulus 1599 hut

hut circles

B 3212

old mine workings

1

car park

68 82 Bennett's Cross 81 68

Route 18. Bennett's Cross, Birch Tor, West Coombe, Leapra Cross, Lettaford, Hurston, Bennett's Cross

A walk which includes fields and lanes as well as open moorland

Distance: 6½ miles
For: Walkers only
Terrain: Moderately difficult
Route-finding: Easy
Maps: 1:25000 sheet SX68/78; 1:50000 sheet 191; 1:63360 Tourist Map

Start: Bennett's Cross car park on the B3212 ½ mile north-east of the Warren House Inn between Moretonhampstead and Postbridge, grid reference SX680818
Parking: There is a small car park at Bennett's Cross
Buses: Western National service 82 Plymouth to Moretonhampstead operates on Saturdays, Sundays, Wednesdays and Bank Holidays during the summer
Refreshments: Snacks are available at the Warren House Inn near the start of the walk

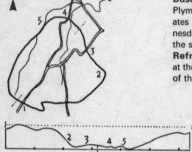

1 From the car park follow the clear track which runs up to Birch Tor, passing a walled enclosure. (The route shown on all Ordnance Survey maps does not exist.) At the top of Birch Tor, turn left and follow the clear path along the ridge until reaching a small roofless turf and stone construction. Turn right and follow a narrow path through the heather which climbs to the top of the ridge and then drops down to the road. On reaching the road cross over near a stone wall and continue forward uphill along a narrow path, keeping about 200 yds from the stone wall on the right. Just as the wall ahead comes into view, the narrow path forks. Take the left-hand fork and walk towards the wall, where you will find a gate in a kink in the wall. Pass through the gate, bear slightly left and walk downhill along a grassy path towards a pool. There are some fine hut circles on either side of the path. Fork right towards the pool and pass through a stone wall at a gatepost. The path then drops down, follows a stream and passes a partly concreted access road which leads to the house on the left. Continue forward until reaching a gate giving access to a roughly metalled road at Westcombe Farm.

2 After passing through the gate, turn left and follow the path signposted 'To Moorgate'. Cross the farmyard and enter an enclosed lane. Pass through a waymarked gate and follow the clear path across the field to a waymarked gatepost. Continue forward, walking parallel to the hedge on your left, to

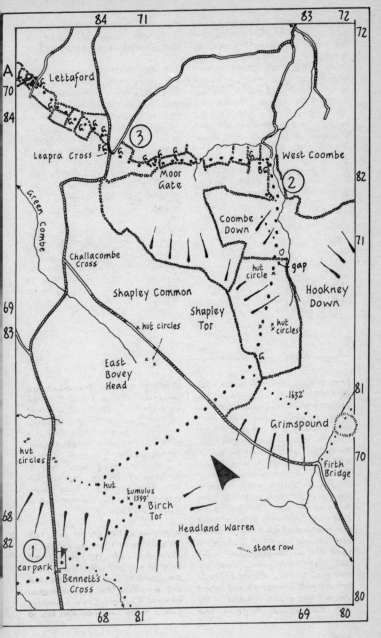

A
70

84

Lettaford

③

Leapra Cross

Green Combe

Moor Gate

West Coombe

Bc

②

82

Challacombe Cross

Coombe Down

Shapley Common

hut circle

gap

Hookney Down

69

83

Shapley Tor

× hut circles

× hut circles

East Bovey Head

G

81

1632'

Grimspound

70

hut circles

hut

Firth Bridge

tumulus
× 1599'

Birch Tor

Headland Warren

68

82

①

car park

Bennett's Cross

stone row

80

reach some trees and a stream. (The gate at the top left-hand corner of the field must be ignored.) Cross the stream, turn left and walk for 30 yds across a boggy patch, climb a stone wall and continue forward along the stream until forced into a meadow. Continue forward to a hedge, turn right and walk to a gate. Turn left through the gate and follow the track to Moorlands. On reaching the house do not enter the farmyard but turn right and walk to a gate. Turn left, follow the edge of the garden to another gate and then turn left to another gate which gives access to the farm drive. Turn right and walk to the gate at the road, noting the cross on the wall of the house at the road.

Turn right along the road and at the first gate by the footpath sign turn left. Bear right and walk to the waymarked gatepost. Bear slightly left, walk parallel to the hedge on your left to another waymarked gatepost and continue forward to a waymarked gate. Go on to another waymarked gate and then to another gate. The path now bears slightly right and runs to a gate leading into a farmyard. Walk through the farmyard to the road at Lettaford.

3

Continued on p. 118

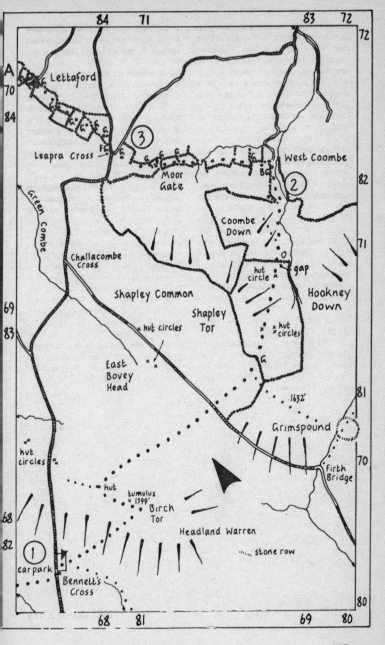

A

Lettaford

Leapra Cross

Green Combe

③

Moor Gate

West Coombe

BC

②

Coombe Down

Challacombe Cross

Shapley Common

Shapley Tor

hut circle ×

gap

Hookney Down

× hut circles

× hut circles

East Bovey Head

× ×

G

1632'

Grimspound

hut circles × ×

hut ×

Firth Bridge

tumulus × 1599'

Birch Tor

Headland Warren

.... stone row

① car park

Bennett's Cross

On emerging from the farmyard continue forward and you will see on your left a footpath sign. Continue along the road, which turns left and becomes an enclosed track. Follow this past a car breaker's yard to a stream, where there is a choice of a ford, footbridge and stepping stones. Turn right and follow the track to the road.

4   At the road turn left and walk uphill to a gate at the end of the farm buildings. There is a footpath sign set high in the hedge. Turn right through the gate, then through another and follow the right-hand headland to the far end of the field, where there is a gate. Pass through the gate and continue forward, following the hedge on your right to a gatepost at the far end of the next field. Continue forward to a stile, then to a gatepost and follow the right-hand headland down the hill to a stile and footpath sign at a lane.

5   Turn left and walk through the farmyard to a footpath sign on the left, pointing towards a gate on the right. Cross the small boggy enclosure to reach the gate and enter an enclosed lane which should be followed across a stream to the road. Cross the stile at a footpath sign, turn left and walk along the road to Lower Hurston. Turn left and follow a track to Higher Hurston. In front of the house, turn right into the farmyard and immediately turn left to enter an enclosed track by means of a gate. Follow the track to some double gates, turn right and follow the right-hand hedge to a gate at the top of the field. Cross a stream and enter an enclosed track which should be followed to a gate which gives access to the open moor.

6   Pass through this gate and follow the wall on your left until it turns left. Aim for the nearest high ground, passing some hut circles not marked on Ordnance Survey maps. On reaching the top of the hill, Fernworthy Forest, a stone circle and a standing stone will be seen on the right. Ahead is a holloway. Make for this and contour the hillside with the valley and the main road on the left. After it turns sharply left and is running directly towards the road, it is crossed by another holloway. At this point, bear slightly right and leave the holloway to follow a narrow but clearly defined path all the way to the road at Bennett's Cross car park.

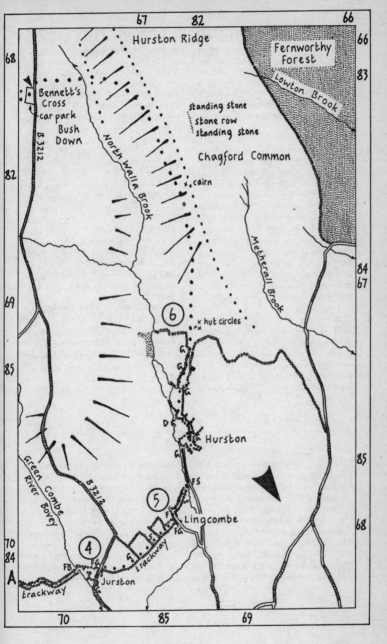

Hurston Ridge

Fernworthy Forest

Lowton Brook

Bennett's Cross
car park
Bush Down

B 3212

North Walla Brook

standing stone
stone row
standing stone

Chagford Common

× cairn

Metherall Brook

⑥ × hut circles
×

Hurston

FS

⑤

Lingcombe

Green Combe
River Bovey

B 3212

④

FB

Jurston

trackway

trackway

Route 19. Postbridge, Fernworthy Forest, Warren House Inn, Pizwell, Postbridge

This route follows the lovely valley of the East Dart and then climbs across open moorland to Fernworthy Forest. From the forest to the Warren House Inn there is a path for a short distance only. The rest of the route is more gentle in character

Distance: 13 miles
For: Walkers and riders
Terrain: Difficult
Route-finding: Difficult – a compass will be useful
Maps: 1:25000 sheets SX67, SX68/78; 1:50000 sheet 191; 1:63360 Tourist Map

Start: The car park in Postbridge on the B3212, grid reference SX645790
Parking: There is a large car park with lavatories and a National Park Information Centre on the north side of the B3212 in the middle of Postbridge
Buses: Western National Service 82 Plymouth to Moretonhampstead operates on Saturdays, Sundays, Wednesdays and Bank Holidays during the summer. National Park Pony Express service 892 Buckfastleigh to Postbridge operates daily during the summer
Refreshments: The public house in Postbridge serves bar snacks. Morning coffee, lunches and afternoon teas are available at the Lydgate House Hotel. The Warren House Inn serves bar snacks

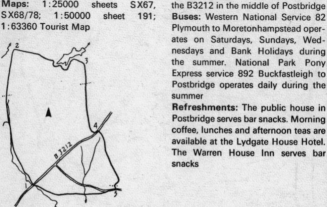

1   From the car park turn left and walk down the road to the bridge. Cross the bridge and immediately turn left, through a gate, and walk to the end of the field, passing through some double gates on the way. At the footpath sign, turn left and walk to the East Dart River. Turn right, pass through two gates and follow the river for about a mile until it bends sharply left at a pleasant grassy spot. Near the

path is a well-preserved beehive hut. It cannot be dated with certainty, as this design has been in use for thousands of years. Continue forward along the tributary stream for a few yards and cross it at a convenient point, turn right and follow the clear path which goes up the hill. (The Ordnance Survey map shows this path running in a straight line through a wet hollow. This is not the correct line.)

Continued on p. 122

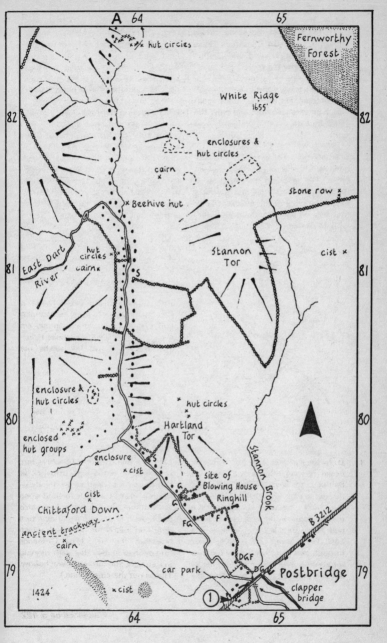

A 64 · 65
Fernworthy Forest
White Ridge 1655'
82 · 82
enclosures & hut circles
×x× hut circles
cairn ×
stone row ×
× Beehive hut
hut circles ×
East Dart River
cairn ×
S
Stannon Tor
cist ×
81 · 81
enclosure & hut circles
enclosed hut groups
× × × ×
enclosure ×
× cist
× hut circles
Hartland Tor
S
80 · 80
cist ×
Chittaford Down
ancient trackway
× cairn
site of Blowing House Ringhill
G
G
FG
F
Stannon Brook
B 3212
DGF
1424'
× cist
car park
DG
Postbridge
clapper bridge
79 · 79
①
64 · 65

Follow the clear path up the hill to reach the fine restored stone circles known as the Grey Wethers. Pass through the gate beyond, bear slightly right and follow the broad path heading for the edge of the forest. Continue forward through a gap in a stone wall and on reaching a broad grassy path which crosses turn right and enter the forest by a gate with a bridleway sign on it.

2   Follow the Forestry Commission gravel track, ignoring the tracks which cross. On reaching the road at a double gate, turn right and follow it round the edge of the reservoir Look for a stile on the left signposted 'Footpath to Reservoir Car Park'. (Riders must continue on the road to the cattle grid.) On reaching the car park, toilets and picnic area (which is beautifully kept and a credit to the Water Authority) walk to the road and turn left. Cross the cattle grid and then turn right to follow the forest boundary.

3   Before leaving the road, take a compass bearing and head due south for about 100 yds. Now search the skyline: you should be able to make out a standing stone with a broad grassy track to the right of it. Walk towards the stone, though you cannot proceed in a direct line because of the fen in the hollow. Keep to the right of this and you will pick up the path.

Continued on p. 124

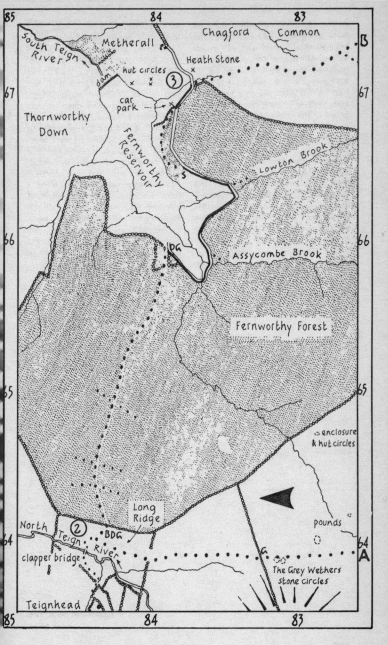

Chagford Common

South Teign River

Metherall

Heath Stone

hut circles

dam

Thornworthy Down

car park

Fernworthy Reservoir

Lowton Brook

Assycombe Brook

Fernworthy Forest

enclosure & hut circles

Long Ridge

pounds

North Teign River

BDG

clapper bridge

The Grey Wethers stone circles

Teignhead

At the top of the hill where the path turns sharp right, turn due south and the standing stone should appear within 40 paces. On reaching the standing stone continue forward for 40 paces and then turn right along a path which gradually gets more distinct until it is very clear and drops down to the Warren House Inn.

4 At the Warren House Inn, turn left and walk along the road until, after 200 yds, you reach on the right a small parking place from where National Park guided walks start. Take the broad track across the moor. Where it forks, bear right and follow the telephone lines to reach the valley bottom by some ruined buildings. Cross the stream and turn right along a clear track to reach the forest edge at a gate. Pass through the gate and continue forward into Soussons Wood. Pass through a boggy patch and almost immediately turn right at a bridleway sign 'Bridlepath to County Road near Soussons Farm'. Pass by the ruins of the Golden Dagger Mines and then turn left to follow a broad forestry road. Where the road bears sharply left, continue forward by a path sign up the hill, following a wide grassy path between the trees. This is signposted at regular intervals until it reaches a gravelled forestry road. Cross this and continue forward downhill to a gate which leads into a field. Go straight on, keeping the forest on your right, to pass through another gate before reaching a gate at Soussons Farm. Pass through this gate and continue forward down the access road to reach a gate which leads on to open country.

Continued on p. 126

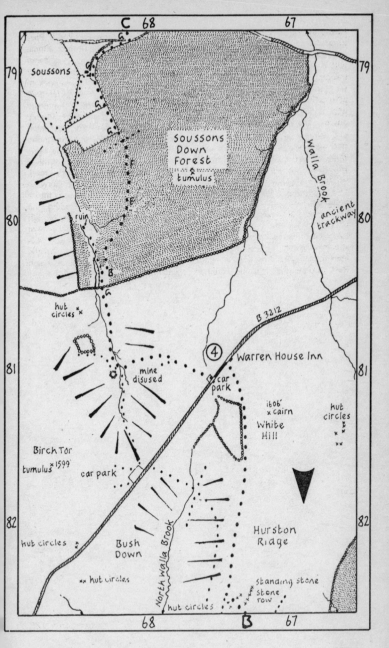

Soussons

Soussons
Down
Forest
x tumulus

Walla Brook

ancient
trackway

ruin

B 3212

hut
circles ×

mine
disused

④ Warren House Inn

car
park

1106'
× cairn

White
Hill

hut
circles
×
× ×

Birch Tor
tumulus × 1599

car park

hut circles ×

Bush
Down

North Walla Brook

×× hut circles

Hurston
Ridge

standing stone
stone
row

hut circles × ×

5 Follow the track all the way to the road and then turn right. Follow the road for ¼ mile until it turns right and then leave it to continue forward along a track which arrives at the farm at Pizwell. Walk between the buildings in the direction indicated by the bridleway sign and at the end of the farm turn left through a gate and, keeping the wall on your left, walk to the wall ahead where there is a footpath sign. *Do not pass through the gate*, but turn right and walk downhill, keeping the wall on your left. Pass through a gate, bear left and make for a signpost near an electricity pole. *Do not enter the enclosed lane ahead*, but keep to the right of a wall built from massive boulders and follow the waymarks to a gate. Continue forward along a sunken grassy path which bears to the left and then reaches a gate by a signpost. Continue forward across the field and at the far end turn left and walk downhill towards the river. Turn right just below a hut and follow the signposts to the Lydgate House Hotel, which can be seen ahead, to reach a metalled lane which will bring you into Postbridge.

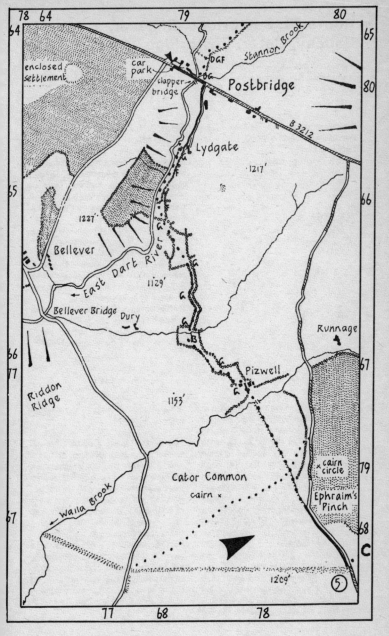

78 64   79   80

64   65

enclosed settlement

DGF

Stannon Brook

car park

OG

clapper bridge

Postbridge

B 3212

Lydgate

1217'

65   66

1227'

Bellever

East Dart River

1129'

← East Dart River

Bellever Bridge Dury

66   Runnage

77

Riddon Ridge

B

Pizwell

67   67

1153'

Walla Brook

Cator Common

cairn ×

cairn circle ×

79

Ephraim's Pinch

67   68

C

⑤

1209'

77   68   78

Route 20. Postbridge, Bellever, Babeny, Cator, Postbridge

A pleasant, relatively level walk through forest, moorland and cultivated countryside. At Laughter Hole House the East Dart River has to be crossed by stepping stones, which may be impossible when the river is in spate

Distance: 8 miles
For: Walkers only
Terrain: Easy
Route-finding: Easy

Maps: 1:25000 sheet SX67; 1:50000 sheet 191; 1:63360 Tourist Map
Start: The car park in Postbridge on the B3212, grid reference SX645790
Parking: Large car park with lavatories and a National Park Information Centre on the north side of the B3212 in the middle of Postbridge
Buses: Western National Service 82 Plymouth to Moretonhampstead operates on summer Saturdays, Sundays, Wednesdays and Bank Holidays. National Park Pony Express service 892 Buckfastleigh to Postbridge operates daily in summer.
Refreshments: The public house in Postbridge serves bar snacks. Morning coffee, lunches and teas are available from the Lydgate House Hotel

1 From the car park on the main road in Postbridge, turn left and walk towards the bridge. Turn right through a gate with a bridleway sign and walk along the river, past the ancient clapper bridge, to a gate. Climb the steep bank and continue forward along a broad grassy path which heads for the road at the far end of the forest on your right. At the road, walk alongside it until it bears right 100 yds before reaching the T-junction at Bellever. Leave the road here and continue forward to the right-hand edge of the forest ahead. Cross the road and follow the Forestry Commission road past a car park and picnic site. (This is a recently diverted path and the Ordnance Survey maps show the old route across the fields to the western edge of Bellever.)

Follow the road, passing through several gates and ignoring all tracks which branch off, to a gate near Laughter Hole Farm. Turn left along a track which follows a wall on the left. After 15 yds, bear right to follow a path through the forest signposted 'Bridlepath to Sherrill via Stepping Stones and Babeny'. At the next signpost 'To Sherrill', turn left and follow a stone wall on the left to a gate on the edge of the garden of Laughter Hole House. Follow the waymarks round the garden fence to the stepping stones across the East Dart River. **2**

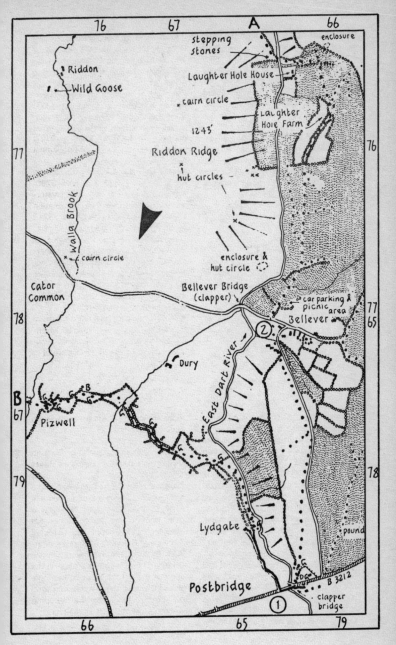

stepping stones

enclosure

Riddon

Wild Goose

Laughter Hole House

cairn circle

1243'

Laughter Hole Farm

Riddon Ridge

hut circles

Walla Brook

cairn circle

enclosure & hut circle

Cator Common

Bellever Bridge (clapper)

car parking & picnic area

Bellever

②

Dury

East Dart River

pound

B

Pizwell

Lydgate

Postbridge

①

clapper bridge

B 3212

Cross the river, pass through the gate, follow the forest edge for a few yards and then continue along the path which bears to the right and ultimately joins the wall on the right at a gate which gives access to an enclosed lane leading to the road near Babeny Farm.

3 Turn left and follow the road to where it curves sharply right near Sherrill Farm (on the right-hand side of the road). On the left is a footpath sign high on the bank pointing along a track marked 'To County Road at Cator Gate'. At the road, turn left until reaching a road junction. Take the road signposted 'To Bellever' until reaching a belt of trees at the top of a slight rise. Turn right through a gate signposted 'Bridlepath to County Road for Runnage Bridge'. Follow the broad, grassy path which moves away from the trees on the right to reach a track at a signpost. Turn right and follow the well-defined track to a gate in a barbed-wire fence.

Continued on p. 132

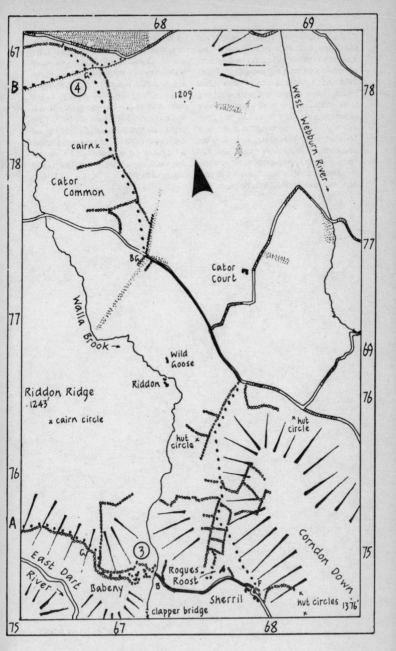

4 Turn left and walk along a wide track across a ford to Pizwell Farm. Walk between the buildings in the direction indicated by the bridleway sign and at the end of the farm turn left through a gate and, keeping the wall on your left, walk to the wall ahead where there is a footpath sign. *Do not pass through the gate*, but turn right and walk downhill, keeping the wall on your left. Pass through a gate, bear left and make for the signpost beside the electricity pole. *Do not enter the enclosed lane ahead*, but keep to the right of a wall built of massive boulders and follow the waymarks to a gate. Continue forward along a sunken grassy path which bears to the left and then reaches a gate by a signpost. Continue forward across the field and at the far end turn left and walk downhill towards the river. Turn right just below a hut and follow the signposts to the Lydgate House Hotel, which can be seen ahead, to reach a metalled lane which will bring you into Postbridge.

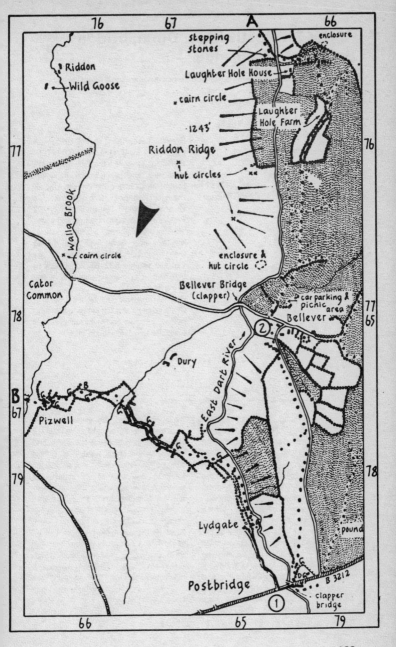

A

stepping
stones

enclosure

Riddon
Wild Goose

Laughter Hole House

cairn circle

Laughter
Hole Farm

·1243·

Riddon Ridge

hut circles

Walla Brook

cairn circle

enclosure &
hut circle

Cator
Common

Bellever Bridge
(clapper)

car parking &
picnic area

Bellever

②

Dury

East Dart River

B

Pizwell

Lydgate

pound

Postbridge

B 3212

clapper
bridge

①

Route 21. Postbridge, Dunnabridge, Bellever, Postbridge

A pleasant level route through forests and across moorland, following clearly defined tracks

Distance: 6 miles
For: Walkers only
Terrain: Easy
Route-finding: Easy
Maps: 1:25000 sheet SX67; 1:50000 sheet 191; 1:63360 Tourist Map

Start: The car park in Postbridge on the B3212, grid reference SX645790
Parking: There is a large car park with lavatories and a National Park Information Centre on the north side of the B3212 in the middle of Postbridge
Buses: Western National service 82 Plymouth to Moretonhampstead operates on Saturdays, Sundays, Wednesdays and Bank Holidays during the summer. National Park Pony Express service 892 Buckfastleigh to Postbridge operates daily during the summer
Refreshments: The public house in Postbridge serves bar snacks. Morning coffee, lunches and teas are available from the Lydgate House Hotel

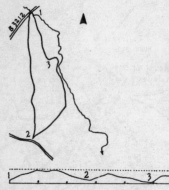

1 Leave the car park and turn right to walk along the B3212 in the direction of Two Bridges. Take the first road on the left and cross a cattle grid. Turn right immediately and pass through some double gates which give access to a gravelled forestry track bearing round to the left. Continue forward, ignoring the gravelled track which runs off to the right, and at the next fork bear right and follow the wider track until reaching a major crossing of tracks. Go straight on, leaving the gravelled track to follow a narrower track signposted to 'Dunnabridge and Huccaby'. On reaching the open moor, continue forward following the track which keeps close to the edge of the wood. (A clear path runs up to Bellever Tor and the views are well worth the diversion and steep climb.) On reaching a stone wall at the end of the wood, turn right and follow the path signposted 'Dunnabridge', keeping the wall on your left. On reaching a wall which runs at right-angles, turn left through a gate and follow the wall which is now on your right. It curves away to the right towards the main road, which can be seen in the distance. Follow the wall until coming to another wall which crosses it. Pass through the gate and continue forward, still keeping the wall on your right. Where the wall turns sharply right, the path goes straight on aiming towards the wall ahead.

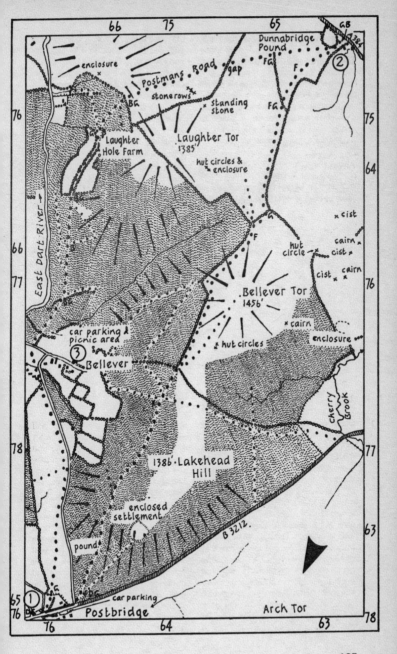

enclosure

66   75   65   GB
384

Dunnabridge
Pound
Postmans Road   gap   FG   F   ②
BG   stonerows   FG
standing
stone
76   Laughter   Laughter Tor   FG   75
Hole Farm   1385'
hut circles &   64
enclosure

East Dart River →

66   cist
hut
circle   cairn
cist   77   F   cist
cist   cairn
76
Bellever Tor
1456'

car parking &   cairn
picnic area   hut circles   enclosure
③   Bellever

78   Cherry Brook

77
1386' Lakehead
Hill

enclosed
settlement   B 3212
63
pound

65   car parking   78
76   ①   Postbridge   Arch Tor
76   64   63

135

2 On reaching the gate near the road, turn back and follow the broad stony track signposted 'To County Road at Bellever'. On reaching the forest at a gate and bridleway sign, walk down the hill, ignoring the wider gravelled track which runs off to the left. Follow the clear track through a series of gates past Laughter Hole Farm to reach the road near a picnic site.

3 Cross the road and continue forward for 100 yds to reach another road. Follow the path which runs close to and parallel to the road as far as the gravelled forestry track. Cross the track and continue close to the road for another 200 yds and then bear slightly right to follow a broad grassy track. On the edge of Postbridge there is a barbed-wire fence and a short descent to a small hunting gate. Follow the clearly defined track, keeping the stone wall on your left, past the clapper bridge to reach the road. Turn left and walk to the car park. (This is a recently diverted path and the Ordnance Survey maps show the old route across the fields from the western edge of Bellever.)

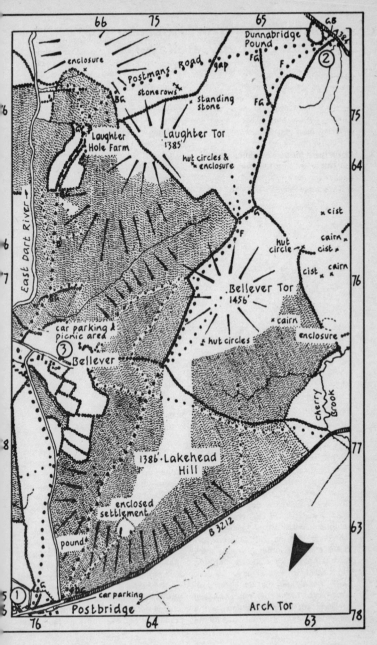

enclosure

Postmans Road

Dunnabridge
Pound

G.B
1384

②

gap

FG

F

BG

stone rows

standing
stone

FG

Laughter Tor
1385'

Laughter
Hole Farm

hut circles &
enclosure

East Dart River

F

hut
circle

cist

cairn

cist

cist

cairn

Bellever Tor
1456'

cairn

enclosure

car parking &
picnic area

③

Bellever

hut circles

Cherry Brook

1388' Lakehead
Hill

enclosed
settlement

pound

B 3212

①

car parking

Postbridge

Arch Tor

Route 22. Bellever, Huccaby Tor, Brimpts, Babeny, Bellever

A fairly level walk through forests and across open moorland

Distance: 7 miles
For: Walkers only
Terrain: Moderately difficult
Route-finding: Moderately difficult

Maps: 1:25000 sheet SX67; 1:50000 sheet 191; 1:63360 Tourist Map
Start: Bellever, 1 mile off the B3212, south-east of Postbridge, grid reference SX655774
Parking: The Forestry Commission car park just east of Bellever, grid reference SX656774
Buses: None. Postbridge, 1 mile distant, is served by Western National service 82 Plymouth to Moretonhampstead on summer Saturdays, Sundays, Wednesdays and Bank Holidays. National Park Pony Express service 892 Buckfastleigh to Postbridge operates daily in summer
Refreshments: Cream teas at Brimpts Farm

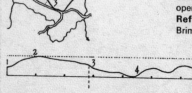

1 Turn left from the car park and walk to the road. Turn left and walk into Bellever, continuing forward at the road junction past the 'No Through Road' sign. The road deteriorates into a track and climbs a hill to a gate and a bridleway sign at the edge of the forest. Pass through the gate, immediately fork left and follow the sign 'To the B3357 via Bellever Tor'. Near the top of the hill, where a broad forestry track comes in from the right, continue forward and at another gravelled track bear left along it for 20 yds, then turn right to climb up a steep stony path with a wall on the left. The path emerges on to the open moor opposite Bellever Tor (worth climbing for the splendid views). Turn left and follow the forest edge to reach a wall and a signpost at the corner of the forest.

Cross the wall and look for a narrow **2** path which goes diagonally across the open moor at an angle which, if projected backwards, would bisect the angle of the two walls (compass bearing 142°). (The path on the Ordnance Survey maps is not visible on the ground and probably never existed.) At a standing stone (which appears as you near the top of the ridge) continue forward to a stone wall and cross it where it is broken. Bear slightly right and look for a path which heads towards a signpost and a broad track. Cross the track and walk towards the conifers on the horizon (compass

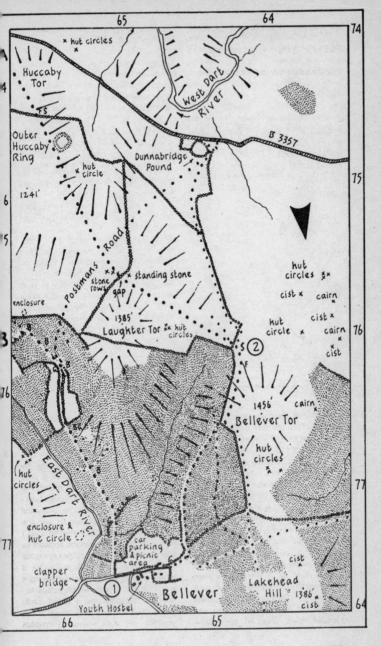

bearing 168°), keeping to the edge of the mine-workings on the right. Suddenly a narrow but well-defined path will appear. (It is worth casting round to find this path.) On the flank of the hill ahead there appear to be two paths. The upper path is correct, the lower being an abandoned leat. Follow it across the moor to a stile and footpath sign in a stone wall. Cross the stile and follow the obvious grassy path to the top of Huccaby Tor, then bear left and walk downhill to reach the road at a gate and footpath sign by a clump of trees. *Now turn to paragraph 3 on p. 142.*

(*Continued from p. 142*) Cross the East Dart River (which may not be possible after heavy rain) and follow the waymarked route around the garden to a gate at the forest edge. Continue forward to a T-junction of tracks, turn right and follow a forest track to reach a gravelled road at Laughter Hole Farm. Turn right and walk about a mile to the car park.

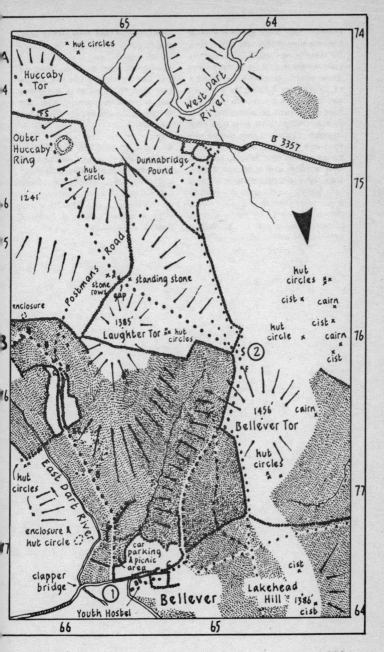

hut circles

Huccaby Tor

West Dart River

Outer Huccaby Ring

TS

Dunnabridge Pound

B 3357

hut circle

1241'

Postmans Road

standing stone

stone rows

gap

hut circles

cist

cairn

enclosure

1385'

Laughter Tor

hut circles

hut circle

cist

cairn

cist

S 2

F

1456'

cairn

Bellever Tor

hut circles

East Dart River

hut circles

enclosure & hut circle

car parking & picnic area

1

clapper bridge

cist

Bellever

Lakehead Hill

1386'

cist

Youth Hostel

3 Turn left and walk along the road. Pass the turn to Hexworthy and look for the sign on the left to Brimpts Farm. Leave the road and follow the access road to Brimpts Farm. Cross a track, continue forward to the farm and then bear left and walk round the back of the farmhouse into the farmyard. Bear slightly left, pass through a waymarked gate and immediately turn right at a path sign and walk down the edge of the field. After 30 yds, turn right through a gate to join a farm track. Turn left, pass through another gate and follow the track downhill to a hunting gate at the river. Pass through the gate and follow a most pleasant riverside path to a bridlepath sign which points across the river.

Cross the East Dart River by the stepping stones (which may be under water when the river is in spate) and continue forward between a stone wall and a stream, a tributary of the East Dart. Turn right at a clapper bridge, cross the stream, bear left through some bushes and make for the road.

At the road, turn left and walk to **4** Babeny Farm. Bear right along a track which goes round the edge of the farm and comes out at the open moor at a gate. Continue forward, following the wall on the left, to go downhill to the stepping stones in front of Laughter Hole House. *Now turn to p. 140.*

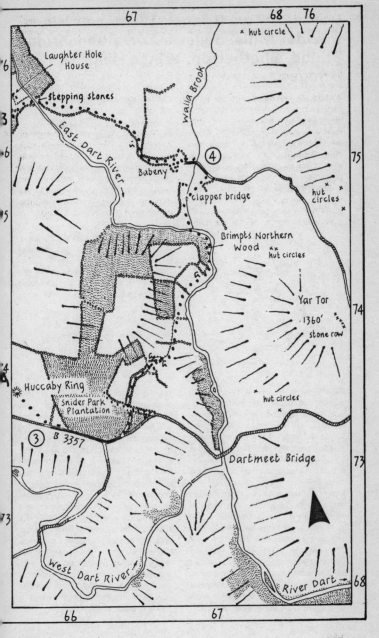

67   68   76

× hut circle

Laughter Hole
House

"6

stepping stones

3

East Dart River

Walla Brook

④

Babeny

clapper bridge

hut circles

75

Brimpts Northern
Wood

× hut circles

Yar Tor

·1360'

stone row

74

hut circles

Huccaby Ring

Snider Park
Plantation

③ B 3357

Dartmeet Bridge

73

73

West Dart River

River Dart

68

66   67

Route 23. Two Bridges, Wistman's Wood, Powder Mills, Bellever Tor, Dunnabridge Pound, Sherberton, Prince Hall, Two Bridges

A fine walk with many contrasts, ranging from wild moorland to gentle valleys

Distance: 10 miles
For: Walkers only
Terrain: Difficult. If the West Dart River is in spate the stepping stones near Sherberton may be difficult to cross

Route-finding: Moderately difficult
Maps: 1:25000 sheet SX67; 1:50000 sheet 191; 1:63360 Tourist Map
Start: Two Bridges at the junction of the B3357 and B3212
Parking: In old quarry opposite the Two Bridges Hotel, grid reference SX 609750
Buses: Western National service 82 operates on Saturdays, Sundays, Wednesdays and Bank Holidays during the summer
Refreshments: Bar snacks at the Two Bridges Hotel, but walkers, unless residents, are not welcomed

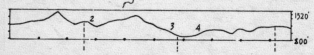

1 Pass through the gate with a footpath sign opposite the Two Bridges Hotel and follow a broad track. At Crockern Cottage, fork right and follow the path round the edge of the boundary wall to a footpath sign directing the walker to Wistman's Wood. The path leaves the stone wall and tends to go away from the river. After about 200 yds leave the main track at a footpath sign and fork left to a stone wall with a stile in it. Cross the stile and follow the path which contours the hillside until reaching a ladder stile in a stone wall. The next part is difficult. On reaching Wistman's Wood, continue forward until exactly opposite the tor next to the one with the flag staff on it (this is on the other side of the river). Now turn right, walk uphill and, on reach-

ing the top of the ridge, aim for the midway point in the line of trees ahead. As you descend the hill a stone wall will come into view. Look for the hunting gate, pass through it and aim for the hunting gate to the left of the trees ahead. There is no path through the fen. Pass through the hunting gate and continue forward to the right of the chimney, which was once used in the manufacture of gunpowder. At a track beside a stream, turn right for 200 yds. Turn left over a clapper bridge, walking towards another chimney. Immediately after crossing the clapper bridge, fork right, pass through a gate in a stone wall with a very tall gatepost and then walk parallel to the barbed-wire fence on the right. (There is a very wet patch in the field.)

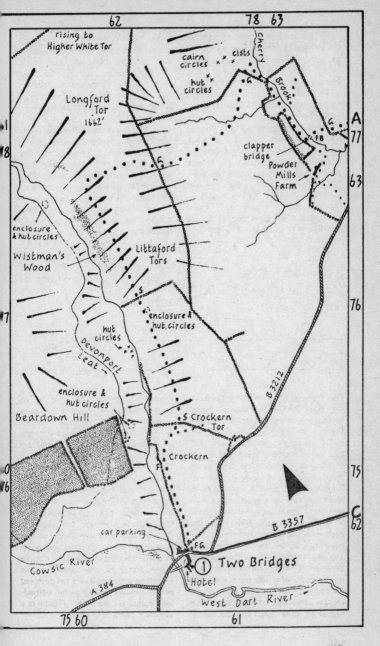

rising to
Higher White Tor

cairn
circles × × cists

Cherry Brook

hut
circles ×

Longford
Tor
1662'

G

G

FB

clapper
bridge

Powder
Mills
Farm

enclosure
& hut circles

Wistman's
Wood

Littaford
Tors

S

enclosure &
hut circles

hut
circles
× × ×

Devonport
Leat

enclosure &
hut circles

Beardown Hill

S Crockern
Tor

Crockern

F

B 3212

car parking

FG

① Two Bridges

Hotel!

Cowsic River

A 384

West Dart River

B 3357

145

2 Cross the road at a gate and follow the ancient Lichway, climbing the hill towards the forest. Enter the forest by a gate, cross a gravelled forestry road and continue forward. Enter the forest again and almost immediately turn right along a path signposted 'To Dunnabridge and Huccaby'. On reaching the open moor at a stone wall and a gatepost, continue forward, keeping the forest on your left. On reaching the end of the plantation, *do not pass through the stone wall*, but follow it, keeping it on the left, following the sign 'To Dunnabridge'. On reaching a stone wall which crosses, turn left, pass through a gate and follow the wall on the right as it curves round to the right. Pass through a gate in the wall which crosses the wall being followed and soon afterwards, where the wall bears round sharply to the right, continue forward by a footpath sign following a track which leads to a gate at the road.

3 Turn left and walk along the right-hand verge, keeping as close to the wall as possible. The wall bears away from the road and drops down to a gate and a bridleway sign. Pass through the gate and walk parallel to the river, following the orange way-marks. On reaching the river bank, turn left and follow it to a footpath sign and stepping stones.

Continued on p. 148

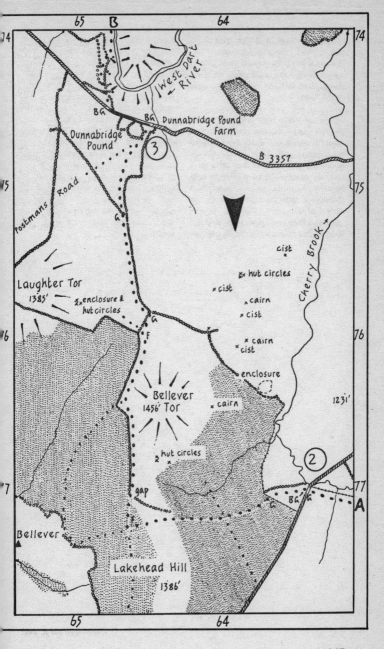

B

West Dart River

BG

BG Dunnabridge Pound Farm

Dunnabridge Pound

③

B 3357

Postmans Road

G

cist
×

×× hut circles

× cist

× cairn

× cist

Laughter Tor

1385'

×× enclosure &
hut circles

G

F

×

× cairn
× cist

enclosure

Bellever
1456' Tor

× cairn

1231'

× hut circles

②

gap

BG

Bellever

A

Lakehead Hill

1386'

Cross the stepping stones (which may not be practicable if the river is in spate) and continue forward, following a tributary stream to a gate in a wall. Turn right, cross some stepping stones, turn left and make for the gate at the road.

4 At the road turn right and walk uphill to the farm. Enter the farmyard through a gate and cross the farmyard to another gate. Turn left and walk uphill through an enclosed lane for a short distance. At the top take the left-hand fork, enter an enclosed lane through a gate and pass through a series of pens. At the end of the enclosed lane is a gate. Pass through it, fork left and walk parallel to the wall on the left, aiming for a junction of walls ahead. There is a small stone circle on the left. Cross the stone wall where it is broken and then continue forward on a compass bearing of 224°. If you have no compass, hold your watch arm exactly parallel to the wall and aim in the direction of 10 past the hour. If you have only a digital watch, or no watch at all, make for the group of boulders ahead. On reaching a broad grassy track, turn right and walk to a gate. Continue forward to a pair of gates. Pass through the one on the right and follow the stone wall on the right to reach the Dartmoor Training Centre. Follow the metalled lane to the road, turn left and walk into Two Bridges.

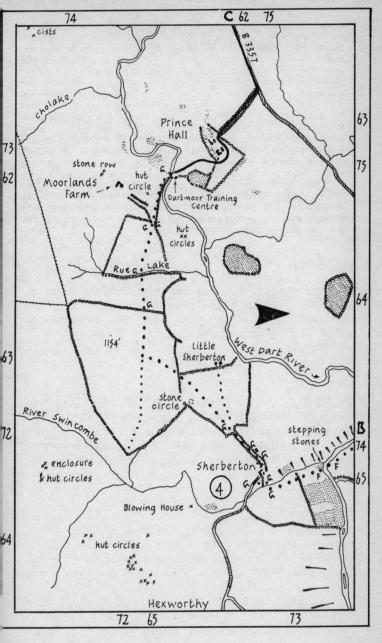

Suggested Outline Routes for Experienced Hill Walkers

These routes have been included for those experienced hill walkers who would like to see something of the wilder parts of the moor. Note that very often there is no path and the walker will need to navigate by compass from tor to tor. In many cases it will be necessary to make detours from the direct line to avoid boggy areas. None of these routes should be attempted in bad weather. Grid references are given so that the route can be plotted on the map.

Route 24

Whiteworks (613710), **Fox Tor** (624698), **Cater's Beam** (631690), **Fishlake** (648681), **Duck's Pool** (623679), **Hen Tor** (593653), **Cuckoo Rock** (588687), **Whiteworks** (613710). 16 miles.

Route 25

Postbridge (645790), **Crow Tor** (607787), **Flat Tor** (604807), **Fur Tor** (588830), **Lints Tor** (580875), **High Willhays** (580893), **Cranmere Pool** (603858), **Quintin's Man** (621838), **Postbridge** (645790). 22 miles. Check that the Merrivale and Okehampton firing ranges are open.

Route 26

Postbridge (645790), **Sandyhole Pass** (623815), **Cranmere Pool** (603858), **Cut Hill** (599828), **Flat Tor** (604807), **Broad Down** (625805), **Postbridge** (645790). 13 miles. Check that the Merrivale and Okehampton firing ranges are open.

Route 27

Ivybridge (637562), **Red Lake** (645664), **Cater's Beam** (631690), **Whiteworks** (613710), **Two Bridges** (610750). 16 miles. This is a linear route and if combined with route 28 will provide a 31-mile route from the southern to the northern edge of the moor.

Route 28

Two Bridges (610750), **Cowsic Head** (594804), **Cut Hill** (599828), **Cranmere Pool** (603858), **Okement Hill** (604875), **Okehampton** (587953). 15 miles. Check that the Merrivale and Okehampton firing ranges are open. This is a linear route and can be combined with route 27 to form a route from one side of Dartmoor to the other.

Index of Place Names

Index of Place Names

Index of Place Names

Find Out More About Penguin Books

We publish the largest range of titles of any English language paperback publisher. As well as novels, crime and science fiction, humour, biography and large-format illustrated books, Penguin series include *Pelican Books* (on the arts, sciences and current affairs), *Penguin Reference Books, Penguin Classics, Penguin Modern Classics, Penguin English Library, Penguin Handbooks* (on subjects from cookery and gardening to sport), and *Puffin Books* for children. Other series cover a wide variety of interests from poetry to crosswords, and there are also several newly formed series – *King Penguin, Penguin American Library*, and *Penguin Travel Library*.

We are an international publishing house, but for copyright reasons not every Penguin title is available in every country. To find out more about the Penguins available in your country please write to our U.K. office – Dept E P, Penguin Books Ltd, Harmondsworth, Middlesex UB7 0DA – unless you live in one of the following areas:

In the U.S.A.: Dept D G, Penguin Books, 299 Murray Hill Parkway, East Rutherford, New Jersey 07073.

In Canada: Penguin Books Canada Ltd, 2801 John Street, Markham, Ontario L3R 1B4.

In Australia: Marketing Department, Penguin Books Australia Ltd, P.O. Box 257, Ringwood, Victoria 3134.

In New Zealand: Marketing Department, Penguin Books (N.Z.) Ltd, P.O. Box 4019, Auckland 10.

In India: Penguin Overseas Ltd, 706 Eros Apartments, 56 Nehru Place, New Delhi 110019.

The Penguin Footpath Guides

H. D. Westacott

Mapped by Hugh Richards

The Brecon Beacons National Park
The Cornwall South Coast Path
The Devon South Coast Path
The Dorset Coast Path
The North Downs Way
The Ridgeway Path
The Somerset and North Devon Coast Path
The South Downs Way

also by H. D. Westacott in Penguins

The Walker's Handbook

Second Enlarged Edition

Maps, tents, clothes, rights of way, National Parks, the law, hostels, farmers, gamekeepers, shoes, boots, safety and first aid – all you need to know to walk safely and happily, whether you take the low road or the high road. This new and enlarged edition also includes extra chapters on challenge walks and walking abroad.